GROWING WITH GOD:
From Cultivation to Harvest

Discipleship Lessons for Kids

MARK AND GLENDA ALPHIN

Growing with God: From Cultivation to Harvest by Mark and Glenda Alphin. This book is a compilation of *Growing with God: Cultivating Growth*, formerly entitled *Growing with God*, and *Growing with God: Encouraging Relationship*, formerly entitled *Growing with God 2*. Copyright © 2014.

All rights reserved including the right of reproduction in whole or in part in any form, except for the inclusion of brief quotations in a review or article, without the prior written permission of the author. Author will allow one exception: permission to copy in part for educational purposes only.

ISBN-10: 1502985446
ISBN-13: 978-1502985446

Cover design by Kim Wood Designs. Photography by Anthony Gates.

Scripture texts and dictionary definitions were obtained through e-Sword, © 2003 Rick Myers. All rights reserved; public domain software. Used by permission.

Scripture quotations marked (KJV) are taken from the 1769 version of the King James Version of the Holy Bible (also known as the Authorized Version); public domain.

Scripture quotations marked (GW) are taken from the © 1995 by GOD'S WORD to the Nations Society. Used by permission.

Scripture quotations marked (BBE) are taken from the 1949/1964 Bible in Basic English. Printed in 1965 by Cambridge Press; public domain.

Scripture quotations marked (CEV) are from the Contemporary English Version Copyright © 1991, 1992, 1995 by American Bible Society, Used by Permission.

Scriptures marked (LITV) are taken from the Literal Translation of the Holy Bible, copyright © 1976-2000 by Jay P. Green, Sr. Used by permission of the copyright holder.

Scriptures quotations marked (MKJV) are taken from the Holy Bible. Scripture taken from the Holy Bible, Modern King James Version Copyright © 1962 – 1998 By Jay P. Green, Sr. Used by permission of the copyright holder.

Scripture quotations marked (NKJV) are taken from the Holy Bible, The New King James Version [computer file].—electronic ed.—Nashville: Thomas Nelson, 1996, c1982.

Scripture quotations marked (WEB) are taken from the Holy Bible. The World English Bible (WEB) is a Public Domain (no copyright) Modern English translation of the Holy Bible, based on the American Standard Version of the Holy Bible first published in 1901, the Biblia Hebraica Stutgartensa Old Testament, and the Greek Majority Text New Testament.

Scripture quotations marked (ASV) are taken from the Holy Bible, 1901 American Standard Version, (Oak Harbor, WA: Logos Research Systems, Inc.), copyright 1994.

Scripture quotations marked (GNT) are taken from the Good News Translation® (Today's English Version, Second Edition) Copyright © 1992 American Bible Society. All rights reserved.

Scripture quotations marked (NLT) are taken from the Holy Bible, New Living Translation copyright © 1996, 2004, 2007, 2013 by Tyndale House Foundation. Used by permission of Tyndale House Publishers Inc., Carol Stream, Illinois 60188. All rights reserved. New Living, NLT, and the New Living Translation logo are registered trademarks of Tyndale House Publishers.

Scriptures marked (EMTV) are taken from the English Majority Text Version (EMTV) of the Holy Bible, New Testament. Copyright © 2002-2003 Paul W. Esposito.

Scripture quotations marked (RSV) are from the New Revised Standard Version Bible, copyright © 1989 the Division of Christian Education of the National Council of the Churches of Christ in the United States of America. Used by permission. All rights reserved.

Scripture quotations marked (NIV) are taken from the Holy Bible, New International Version, © 1973, 1978, 1984 by the International Bible Society.

DEDICATION

To our gifts from God, Miranda and Candace

Our lives have gone through much change since the *Growing with God* journey began back in 2003. Miranda, you married your prince, Stefan, and your ministry as a married couple is already flourishing. We are so thankful for all that the Lord has done, and we will continue to watch and pray as you and Stefan traverse life's path together. Candace, who knew that when God called you to missions at age 5, you would be our "right-hand girl" in ministry on a foreign field? His ways never cease to amaze us!

We love you, and always remember that *we believe in you*, and *Jesus does, too.*

Dad and Mom

CONTENTS

ACKNOWLEDGMENTS i
PREFACE iii
Children in the Bible 3
Why did God Make Me? 4
What is Sin? 6
Sin: Can I Kick the Habit? 8
What is repentance? 10
Let's Explore Baptism! 12
The Holy Ghost (What is it?) 15
Do I Need the Holy Ghost? 16
How Soft is Your Dirt? 19
Being Consistent in All Things 22
How Can I Gain Forgiveness? 24
"To-Do List" Priority #1: Work on My Relationship with God 26
Prayer: Developing our Relationship with God (1) 28
Prayer: Developing our Relationship with God (2) 30
The Eight Areas of Prayer: Introduction to the Prayer Wheel 32
How do I show Praise to God? 35
Consider the Spider 37
Hearing God's Voice 39
What is Intercession? 41
Our Spiritual Ice Cream Sundae: Exploring the Fruits of the Spirit 44
Living a Fruit-Full Life 47
Putting on the Armor of God 49
Temptation: Can We Stand Against It? 51
What Does it Mean to Be Holy? 53
Our Actions: Right or Wrong? 55
Attitude: Right or Wrong, We All Have One! 57
What is My "Holiness Grade?" 59
How Do I Keep My River Flowing? 63
How Can I Make My Time with God Even Better? 65
Becoming a Journalist for Jesus 66
(You + Me) + Working Together = Unity 68
Disobedience vs. Obedience: How does God view them? 70
Having Honor and Respect for Others 72
Integrity: What Is It, and Do I Have to Have It? 73
What Kind of Example are You? 75

I'm Called to be a Soulwinner!	77
Would Jesus Play with My Friends?	79
Two Plans for Your Life	83
What is the Rapture?	86
Heaven or Hell: What's Your Destination?	89
What is Love?	91
Since God is Love, is There Anything He Hates?	94
You Want Me to FAST? But, I'm Just a KID!	96
Why Do We Give Tithes and Offerings?	98
Faith – Something that We Cannot See	100
Will God Heal Us?	102
How Much Faith Do We Need?	104
Faith and Trust: Are They the Same Thing?	106
Praying for Others: The Laying on of Hands: How, Why, and When	108
Gifts of the Spirit, Lesson #1: "Showing" Gifts	111
Gifts of the Spirit, Lesson #2: "Telling" and "Doing" Gifts	114
What does "God is my Father" Mean?	117
Godhead Lesson #1: There is One God	119
Godhead Lesson #2: Jesus is God	122
Godhead Lesson #3: Why is the Name of Jesus so Important?	124
Shame Lesson #1: What is Shame?	132
Shame Lesson #2: How Shame Affects Our Relationships	135
Shame Lesson #3: How Can Shame Mess Up Our Lives?	137
Shame Lesson #4: How Does Shame Affect Me?	140
Teacher's Toolbox	143
ABOUT THE AUTHORS	153

ACKNOWLEDGMENTS

Creating a compilation of the *Growing with God* lessons has been a dream of ours for years, and it's exciting to have finally accomplished the goal. First, to the One, True, and Almighty God whose Name is **JESUS**, thank You for everything that You have bestowed upon us since we began our ministry journey. Above all else, our heart's desire is to please You in everything we do. **Sharon Metzger**, your help was invaluable in helping us accomplish the task. Thank you for all that you've done for us. **Bishop (Pastor) William Sciscoe**, your continued support and covering through prayer has been a rock that we've symbolically leaned upon many times. Mere words cannot express how much we love and appreciate you. **Miranda and Candace**, you were the catalyst that began our ministry. Thank you for the never-ending motivation to share Jesus with others. We love you and believe in you. **Mom and Dad Sword**, you've made sure that our shipments made it to their destination. Thank you for being our help from afar. We honor and appreciate you.

PREFACE

The lessons contained in this book are a compilation of *Growing with God: Cultivating Growth* and *Growing with God: Expanding Relationship*. The material contained herein was written with the purpose of building upon a basic spiritual foundation. After watching the declination in the spirituality of teenagers within our movement, it became clear that many likely do not have a clear understanding of the belief system that had been modeled by their parents or teachers. Subsequently, many teens have chosen to set aside any form of Christianity, choosing rather to follow a "feels good" lifestyle.

The *Growing with God* books were birthed out of a desire to help our own children receive a firm, apostolic doctrinal foundation. God saw that desire and chose to exploit it for His purpose, calling upon us to teach the children within our local assembly as well. The curriculum that you hold in your hand is an ending result to that calling. We have attempted to include information that is necessary for developing a deeper relationship with God, and by deeper, we mean one that goes well beyond "the basics."

We invite you to move beyond the norm. Take this resource and use it to build strong, apostolic-minded Christian character within the children that you love and teach. As parents, we can tell you that it works. Both of our daughters fulfilled what we had internally hoped for, as they are both involved in ministries that extend well beyond our influence. Their relationships with God are grounded in apostolic doctrine that they are ready to share with others, simply because they understand what they believe.

Always remember, God is faithful to help us as long as our goals match His, for He wants everyone to join in the inheritance of His coming Kingdom.

Mark and Glenda Alphin, Authors

Growing with God: Cultivating Growth
Growing with God: Expanding Relationship
Growing with God: From Cultivation to Harvest (compilation)

MARK & GLENDA ALPHIN

PART I

Relationship with God

Relationships with Others

And one of the scribes came, and having heard them reasoning together, and perceiving that he had answered them well, asked him, Which is the first commandment of all?

And Jesus answered him, The first of all the commandments is, Hear, O Israel; The Lord our God is one Lord:

And thou shalt love the Lord thy God with all thy heart, and with all thy soul, and with all thy mind, and with all thy strength: this is the first commandment.

And the second is like, namely this, Thou shalt love thy neighbour as thyself. There is none other commandment greater than these.

(Mark 12:28-31 KJV)

CHILDREN IN THE BIBLE

Lesson suggestion: Gather a few "dress-up" garments so that you can have a few helpers dress up as you talk about the examples. Note: there are multiple Bible characters listed; this makes the lesson easily retaught. Choose one or two examples and simply expand them, telling the story in your own words. The point of the lesson is to prove to the child how important they are to God.

How important are children to God?

We often hear about Gideon, Joshua, Peter, James and John or other adults. What are some examples of children that God used in His Kingdom?

Miriam	Watched over Moses **(Exodus 2:4-9)**
Samuel	Your age when he lived in the temple **(1 Samuel 1:20-28)**
David	Shepherd when Samuel anointed him king over Israel **(1 Samuel 16:11-23)**
Servant girl	Naaman's leprosy **(2 Kings 5:1-14)**
Josiah	King at age 8 **(2 Kings 22:1-2)**
The lad	Gave 5 barley loaves & 2 fishes **(John 6:5-13)** (Barley was the food of poor people.)

Jesus wanted to spend time with children. The Bible tells us how the disciples tried to send away the children who were coming to see Jesus. It upset Him so much that Jesus told everyone that they had to believe like a child to even get into heaven! **(Matthew 18:3-6; 19:13-14; 18:15-17)**

"People were bringing little children to Jesus to have him touch them, but the disciples rebuked them. When Jesus saw this, he was indignant. He said to them, 'Let the little children come to me, and do not hinder them, for the kingdom of God belongs to such as these. I tell you the truth, anyone who will not receive the kingdom of God like a little child will never enter it.' And he took the children in his arms, put his hands on them, and blessed them." **(Mark 10:13–16 NIV)**

When His disciples argued about whom would be the greatest in the kingdom, Jesus used a child to show what it would take to even be a part of it! **(Mark 9:33-37)** God wanted everyone to know how important children are to Him. In fact, Jesus felt it was so important that He had Peter mention them on the Day of Pentecost. **(Acts 2:39 KJV)** *"The promise is unto you and your children..."*

God has a plan for each of you. You are important to Him, and He loves you very much. If you ever feel insignificant, remember this lesson and know that God will use you if you make yourself available to Him. Whatever your future task for Him may be, always remember that **you are important!**

WHY DID GOD MAKE ME?

Lesson suggestion: Whiteboard, markers.

Have you ever wondered why God made you? We are told that we are special to Him, but why? Maybe you don't feel very special, or just don't know what you can do that would get God's interest. Let's look at the Bible and see if we can figure out why we were created.

God created all things. (Genesis 1:1)
We know from the Bible that nothing "just happened." God created everything! **(Colossians 1:16)** Did you know that everything God made has a purpose? You learn in school that the moon not only gives us light at night, but it also controls the tides in the oceans. Rain waters the ground so that plants can grow. Without bees to carry pollen from flower to flower, trees would not bear fruit. We must have a reason for being here. What is it? What makes us different from everything else?

God spoke, and it was. (Genesis 1:3, 6, 14, 21)
When God wanted light, He simply said, *"Let there be light."* He spoke and dry land, the stars, and the animals were created. Can you imagine how awesome that must have been? When God wanted to create something, He just said, *"Let there be...,"* and it was so! That is, except for man, because God made Adam with His own hand, and in His very own image! We are the only part of creation that God did not speak into existence. **(Genesis 1:26-27; 2:7)** God came to earth, took dirt, and formed man with His own hands. Have you ever tried to make a man out of modeling clay? Could you put the amount of detail in that clay man that God put into you? Look at your body. Did you know that God knows how many hairs you have on your head? Why do you think God took so much time when He created you?

We have a soul. (Genesis 2:7)
God did not only make us by hand, but He gave us His breath, and He gave us a soul. Without one, you could not go to heaven. When you die, your life would simply end. God gave us a soul because He wanted us to go to heaven and be with Him forever. No other part of creation has a soul; only we have the promise of eternal life with Jesus

God gave us a choice to obey Him. (Genesis 2:16-17)
God gave us the ability to make choices, and He hopes that we will choose to serve Him. The angels have no choice. When Satan rebelled, there was no way for him to change and return to heaven. God allows us to repent of our sins, and He *will* forgive us, because He wants us to choose to go to heaven to live with Him.

The greatest commandments: to love God and man. (Matthew 22:36-40; Mark 12:28-34)
Love is so important that Jesus said these two commandments are the basis of all others. This means that if you love God and others, you will not want to do the things that the other eight commandments mention. Would you kill someone you love? No! Would you lie to someone you love? No (or you shouldn't)! When you truly love someone, you will not do *anything* to hurt them.

What does it mean to love? (1 Corinthians 13:1-13)
Chapter 13 of 1 Corinthians talks about love. The Bible says that "God is love." If God is love, how can we not love others, yet still say that we are His children? Another scripture in the Bible states, *"By this shall all men know you are My disciples."* **(John 13:35 KJV)** 1 Corinthians 13 talks about wonderful things like miracles, tongues, prophecy (the telling of future events), etc. All of these things are worthless without love. We can have great success, but if we do not have love, then our success is useless.

(John 3:16) God loved us so much that He endured a cruel death in order to save us from our sins. How much do you love *Him*? Let's look at some synonyms (words that mean the same, or almost the same) for love: commitment, affection, tenderness, and to treasure.

Are we committed to God? (Committed means to be obligated to something, such as being committed to keeping our room clean every day!)

> **(Psalms 63:1):** *"Early will I seek thee..."* **(KJV)**
> **(Hebrews 11):** Many were willing to give their lives for their faith in God.
> **(2 Corinthians 11:23-33):** Paul made many sacrifices for God. Can you imagine being shipwrecked, beaten, or put in prison?

Do we feel affection for God? (Luke 1:46-47) Affection is a tender feeling that you have for someone or something, such as a parent or a pet. If we are supposed to love our enemies, how much more affection should we show toward God? In fact, if we do not love God, it will be impossible to love our enemies. **(Luke 6:27)**

Do we have tenderness towards others? (Tenderness means to treat someone with kindness or special regard. Tender: easily crushed or bruised: FRAGILE)[1] Are you kind to other people? **(Ephesians 4:32)**

Where is your treasure? (Treasure: accumulated or hidden wealth in the form of valuables, such as money or jewels)[2] **(Matthew 6:19-21)** Jesus said that your heart would be with your treasure. Is your treasure a new toy, video game, or your friends? Or, does your treasure lie with Jesus? He tells us to put our treasures in heaven with Him.

Did you know that although the angels stand and worship at the throne of God, the Bible says nothing about them being able to love Him? God chose to give us the opportunity to have a special relationship with Him. We are the only part of creation that God loves. **(John 3:16)** In fact, He died on the cross to offer salvation to us. If we truly love him, we will be glad to obey His commandments!

---

[1] Webster's II New Riverside Dictionary, pg. 1192.
[2] Webster's II New Riverside Dictionary, pg. 1230.

WHAT IS SIN?

Lesson suggestion: *Find Bible character pictures (such as provided in Sunday School literature) to use for visual aids while speaking about the different examples supplied for this lesson. Another idea: Cut a big heart out of red construction paper. As you speak of the different sins, use a black marker to make X's on the heart to show the mark that sin leaves on your life. Explain that only by following the plan of salvation can sin be completely removed (repentance brings forgiveness, but sin is removed only after baptism). (Author's note: we realize that the number of biblical examples provided is too many for one sitting; however, we found that we would re-teach our lessons as we gained new students. This allows variety that keeps the lesson interesting for everyone. Choose what is appropriate for you at any given time!)*

Today, we are going to talk about sin. How many of you know what it means to sin?

Sin is disobeying God's laws. **Romans 3:23** says, *"For all have sinned, and come short of the glory of God." ***(KJV)** What will happen if we sin?

The Bible tells us what will happen to us, whether we choose to serve God or live a life of sin. *"For the wages of sin is death; but the gift of God is eternal life through Jesus Christ our Lord."* **(Romans 6:23 KJV)** "Death" does not necessarily mean that you will immediately die if you do something wrong. This just means that a person who chooses to live a life of sin will end up dying a spiritual death. In other words, they will live apart from God, eventually living an eternal life in Hell.

Sin separates us from God. *"But your iniquities have separated between you and your God, and your sins have hid his face from you, that he will not hear."* **(Isaiah 59:2 NLT)** *"But there is a problem — your sins have cut you off from God. Because of your sin, he has turned away and will not listen anymore."* **(KJV)**

Sin is the root (or cause) of many diseases:

Smoking cigarettes can cause different kinds of cancers, especially in the lungs.

Drinking alcohol can cause different kinds of cancers, especially in the liver.

Drugs can cause the brain to work improperly, causing a person to forget important things they have learned.

Dishonesty (lying) can cause anxiety, which can cause upset stomachs. A dishonest person may not be able to sleep or eat well, and cry very easily.

Biblical examples that show the consequences (or results) of sin

Cain: He murdered his brother, Abel. Because of his sin, God banished Cain from his home and made him a wanderer. **(Genesis 4:8-12)**

The Flood: The people in Noah's day were so wicked that God decided to destroy everyone who was not righteous. Noah's family members were the only survivors. **(Genesis 6:5-22)**

Israelites at Mount Horeb: The golden calf that they created upset God so much that He wanted to destroy them! Moses had to ask God not to do this to His people. **(Exodus 32:1-10)**

Sodom and Gomorrah: The destruction of these two cities was a direct result of the sins committed by the people who lived there. **(Genesis 19:24-25)**

Lot's wife: Because Lot's wife would not choose to turn from her life of sin, and looked back with longing at Sodom and Gomorrah, she turned into a pillar of salt. **(Genesis 19:26)**

Moses and Aaron: They did not follow God's exact instructions when He chose to provide water for the complaining Israelites. Because of this, Moses and Aaron were not allowed to enter the Promised Land. **(Numbers 20:1-13)**

Judas: He betrayed Jesus and went against everything that he knew was right. During Jesus' trial, Judas realized he had made a mistake, but in his mind, it was already too late; he believed that there was no hope for him. Judas hanged himself, not understanding that Jesus would have forgiven him if Judas had simply repented of his actions. **(Matthew 27:3-5; Mark 14:43-46)**

Parable of the Wedding Garment: There was a wedding feast, and the master had given all of the guests a special garment to wear. But, one of the guests would not wear his special clothes to dinner! Because of this, the master had him taken away from the feast. **(Matthew 22:11-14)**

Lazarus and the rich man: The rich man would not recognize Lazarus' need for food and comfort. When both men died, Lazarus went to Abraham's bosom, and the rich man went to hell. The rich man wanted Lazarus to go and warn his brothers (for they were most likely very wicked, too), but God would not allow Lazarus to go. **(Luke 16:19-31)**

Peter: Jesus had told Peter that he would deny that he knew Him. And, just as Jesus had said, Peter did do this! It was a very sad thing; however, Peter realized his error, repented, and Jesus forgave him. As we all know, Peter was the mighty preacher who spoke on the day of Pentecost. He was also the first to proclaim the doctrine of repentance, baptism in Jesus name, and receiving the gift of the Holy Ghost! **(John 18:15-17, 25-27)**

We are human, and we will always make mistakes. Because it is our nature to sin, we must continually ask God's forgiveness. **(Psalm 51:5)** However, Jesus is always faithful to forgive us if we ask Him to do so. *"If we confess our sins, He is faithful and just to forgive us our sins, and to cleanse us from all unrighteousness."* **(1 John 1:9 KJV)**

(Colossians 3:24-25) Just as God will punish the unjust, He will also reward those who obey His word and are faithful. We may receive a punishment for actions done here on earth (from a parent or guardian, etc.). However, if we repent and continue to follow what we know is right, God will reward us, both here on earth and in heaven.

SIN: CAN I KICK THE HABIT?

Lesson suggestion: Whiteboard, markers.

One of the first lessons that we learned when we first began studying together was, "What is sin?" We know that God hates sin, so let's look at the Bible and see if we can learn how to avoid (or stay away from) sinning.

Review: Sin is disobeying God's laws. *"For all have sinned, and come short of the glory of God."* **(Romans 3:23 KJV)** *"For the wages of sin is death; but the gift of God is eternal life through Jesus Christ our Lord."* **(Romans 6:23 KJV)**

If we were born sinners, how can we live a life that is free from sin? Is this even possible? (To live without sin means to obey God; to live above sin.) Many believe that Jesus was the only one who was able to do this, but actually, the Bible mentions a few others, too.

Are there examples in the Bible of people who lived without sin?

Enoch (Genesis 5:24; Hebrews 11:5). It is not possible to live a sinful life, yet also have a testimony that says you please God. Also, how is it possible for someone to live a sinless life without the Holy Ghost? The Bible speaks of several that managed to do just that.

The story of Enoch is very interesting. **Hebrews 11:5** says, *"Faith enabled Enoch to be taken instead of dying. No one could find him, because God had taken him. Scripture states that before Enoch was taken, God was pleased with him."* **(GW)**

Adam, the first man on earth, was alive during the first 310 years of Enoch's life. As a matter of fact, Adam was Enoch's great-great-great-great grandfather! Can you imagine the stories that Enoch must have heard about the Garden of Eden? About how Adam walked with God in the cool of the day, naming the animals, and so much more? Enoch may have even seen the angels that guarded the garden!

While the Bible does not plainly state that Enoch lived without sin, it is evident that he lived righteously, so much so that God was pleased with him, and wanted to take Enoch to heaven to be with Him!

Job (Job 1:1-22). These verses talk about the conversations that Satan had with God, and how God allowed Satan to test Job. *"In all this, Job sinned not..."* **(Job 1:22 KJV)** God allowed Job to go through an extreme test to prove to Satan that Job would not forsake Him. God allowed Satan to take all of his possessions, all of his children, and even let Satan make Job very sick. However, Job would not curse (or blame) God because he knew that God was faithful. Did you know that after this test, God blessed Job with twice as much as he had before everything "bad" happened?

Jesus (Hebrews 4:15). Yes, Jesus was God in flesh (He took on the form of a human body. But, do you realize that while living on earth, Jesus chose to live a sinless life? He could have done anything He wanted to do. Satan tempted Him just like he tempts us, but Jesus refused, and even quoted scripture when He resisted (or refused) the temptation.

Cornelius (Acts 10:1-2, 22) (Verse 2: devout = godly; verse 22: just = innocent, holy, righteous). Cornelius did a better job at being a Christian than many "Christians" today. His devotion to God was so strong that God sent an angel to tell Cornelius to send for Peter, and bring him to his house. Remember, Cornelius did not have the Holy Ghost when he saw the angel. His desire to serve God was so strong that the Lord could not just ignore him, making Cornelius wait for the New Testament Church to find him! Rather, God had to make sure that Cornelius learned about the Truth found in scripture, and how to receive salvation!

Paul (2 Timothy 4:7-8). After his conversion, Paul worked very hard and did all he could to spread the gospel. Paul is considered to be the greatest evangelist of the Bible, preaching the gospel of Jesus to most of the known (already-discovered) world during the last one-third of his life.

How can I live without sin?

Prayer: Prayer is talking with God. This is when He will talk to you about changes that you need to make in your life, and how you can achieve them (or make them happen). Without talking to God, how will you know what He wants you to do to help "grow" His church? **(Matthew 26:41; Mark 14:38; 1 Thessalonians 5:17)**

Fasting: Fasting proves to your body that you are in control. It also gives our spirit power over our flesh (it shows the devil that we intend to follow God). Our body doesn't like to go without food for very long before it starts grumbling about it! As children, you can't go on long fasts like adults; your body is growing, and you need the energy and nourishment that you get from food. However, you could probably fast one meal a day, or choose to fast at least one thing for an extended period of time (e.g. candy, soda, video games, or movies). **(Nehemiah 9:1-2; Isaiah 58:6; Jonah 3:5)**

Bible Study: You will learn more about God as you read and study your Bible. Your faith will increase when you read about the many miracles He performed! God's love and power is shown in the things that He did while He was on the earth. Listen to your Sunday School teachers when they encourage you to learn your weekly memory verses! By memorizing scripture, you will obtain ammunition (or power) to use in the war against sin. The Word of God is our most powerful weapon against the devil. Satan is scared of God's Word! **(Psalm 119:11; 2 Timothy 2:15)**

Obedience to God's Word: When we obey God's Word, it gives us strength in our battle against sin. A person can't perform two opposite actions at the same time. Can you turn your head to the left while looking right? No, you can't! We choose to either obey, or to disobey. If we always obey God's Word, we will never fall to sin. **(Jeremiah 7:23; Revelations 3:10)**

Witnessing: *"Dear brothers and sisters, you are foreigners and aliens here. So I warn you to keep away from evil desires because they fight against your very souls. Be careful how you live among your unbelieving neighbors. Even if they accuse you of doing wrong, they will see your honorable behavior, and they will believe and give honor to God when he comes to judge the world."* ***(1 Peter 2:11-12 NLT)***

(1 Peter 3:15-17 NLT) *"Instead, you must worship Christ as Lord of your life. And if you are asked about your Christian hope, always be ready to explain it. But you must do this in a gentle and respectful way. Keep your conscience clear. Then if people speak evil against you, they will be ashamed when they see what a good life you live because you belong to Christ. Remember, it is better to suffer for doing good, if that is what God wants, than to suffer for doing wrong!"*

If you are fulfilling the Great Commission and witnessing to your friends **(Matthew 18:19; Mark 16:15)**, you will be careful not to fail in front of them. You will not want to do anything that will hurt your ability to win them to Jesus.

How can we keep from sinning? We must get as close to Jesus as possible. How do we do this? Through prayer, fasting, studying the Bible, obedience to His Word, and witnessing to others! Isn't it interesting that the very things that help us live a life above (or without) sin will bring us close to Jesus? Sharing Him with others will be much easier to do, for Jesus will always be with you!

WHAT IS REPENTANCE?

Lesson suggestion: Whiteboard, markers. We suggest using a simple illustration to show the effects of sin, such as drawing a heart. Black marks can be made within it and then erased to show the effects of repentance.

What is repentance? (2 Corinthians 7:9-10) Is it simply feeling sorry for the bad things that you have done? Although you feel sorry for your sins, that is not repentance. *(Interact with class in order to make sure that every child understands the difference between repentance and asking for forgiveness.)* How many times have you been scolded by your parent for teasing your brother, sister, or friend, and then been required to apologize, or to ask for forgiveness? If you repeated the behavior, did you really repent, or were you simply asking for forgiveness?

Repentance is a change of heart. Let's look at two different versions of **Acts 2:38**. *"Then Peter said unto them, Repent, and be baptized every one of you in the name of Jesus Christ for the remission of sins, and ye shall receive the gift of the Holy Ghost."* **(KJV)** *"Peter replied, "Each of you must turn from your sins and turn to God, and be baptized in the name of Jesus Christ for the forgiveness of your sins. Then you will receive the gift of the Holy Spirit."* **(NLT)** Have you repented of the things you've done that you know made God unhappy? Or, have you simply asked Him to forgive you? Although we may naturally feel sad that we have wronged God, that is not repentance. Repentance is a change of direction.

Biblical examples of men who had a change of heart

Esau (Genesis 27:41): Esau hated his brother, Jacob, for stealing his blessing from Isaac, their father. Esau vowed to kill Jacob, causing Jacob to flee for his life. Many years later, when Jacob met Esau once again, his brother accepted him; Esau no longer wanted to take Jacob's life. **(Genesis 33:4)** *(Study note: Esau embraced Jacob (v. 4): He ran to meet him, not in passion, but in love; and, as one heartily reconciled to him, he received him with all the endearments imaginable, embraced him, fell on his neck, and kissed him. Some think that when Esau came out to meet Jacob it was with no bad design, but that he brought his 400 men only for state, that he might pay so much the greater respect to his returning brother.[3] They both wept. Jacob wept for joy, to be thus kindly received by his brother whom he had feared; and Esau perhaps wept for grief and shame, to think of the bad design he had conceived against his brother, which he found himself strangely and unaccountably prevented from executing.[4])*

Saul (Acts 22:3): Saul lived his life faultlessly (with no blame), loved God with all of his heart, and obeyed the law exactly as it was written. Saul was a Pharisee who followed the teachings of the Old Testament. The Christians were preaching that Jesus was the Messiah, and Saul believed that this teaching was in direct conflict with the laws of Moses. **(Deuteronomy 13:6-10)** God had to literally knock Saul down and blind him to get his attention! **(Acts 9:1-8)** Saul had not broken any of God's laws, but he did not understand that the Christians were actually worshipping the same God as he. So, how did Saul repent? He changed his heart. **(Acts 22:4-16)** Saul changed from persecuting the Christians to being a Christian himself, and soon became one of the greatest apostles that ever lived. *(Study note: He was zealous against everything that the law prohibited, and for everything that the law enjoined; and this was zeal towards God, because he thought it was for the honor of God and the service of his interests.[5])*

---

[3] Henry, Matthew, Matthew Henry's Commentary on the Bible, (Peabody, MA: Hendrickson Publishers), 1997.
[4] Henry, Matthew, Matthew Henry's Commentary on the Bible, (Peabody, MA: Hendrickson Publishers), 1997.
[5] Henry, Matthew, Matthew Henry's Commentary on the Bible, (Peabody, MA: Hendrickson Publishers), 1997.

How do we repent? We ask God to clean our hearts, and to forgive us for things we have done that have either displeased or made Him sad. Then, we show that we have repented by doing our best never to do the things that make God unhappy. We change our actions and attitudes, which then changes our heart. A change of heart shows true repentance!

LET'S EXPLORE BAPTISM!

Lesson suggestion: Gather the following items together for use in an object lesson: a small doll, small bag of dirt, bowl, container of water, and some clean doll clothes. Prior to class, make sure the doll is noticeably dirty, but not so much so that a "baptism" wouldn't remove the "stains." (See the explanation towards the lesson's end).

We have learned about repentance and why it is necessary for us to repent. Now, we are going to explore baptism! Satan loves to cause disagreements about this subject, because he doesn't want anyone to know and understand the truth that is found in the Bible. Let's study baptism and see if we can figure out why Satan would not want you to be baptized in Jesus' name!

What is baptism?

Did you know that Christians are not the only people to use baptism in their religion? Let's look at what the dictionary says about baptism: "A Christian sacrament marked by symbolic use of water to rid the recipient of original sin and resulting in admission into Christianity. b. A ceremony, trial, or experience by which one is initiated, purified, or given a name."[6]

Baptism is an act (or experience) that purifies us. The Bible says that Jesus is coming back for a bride who is without spot or wrinkle. **(Ephesians 5:27)** We wash clothes to get rid of the spots. So, does baptism accomplish the same thing?

Why do we baptize?

We baptize to follow Jesus' example, for He was baptized by John. (Matthew 3:13-15) Jesus is the greatest example of how we should live. He needed to be baptized to fulfill His righteousness, so we should do the same!

It represents the death of Christ, for our sinful nature (old man) "dies" when we go down into the water. *"Don't you know that all who share in Christ Jesus by being baptized also share in his death? When we were baptized, we died and were buried with Christ. We were baptized, so that we would live a new life, as Christ was raised to life by the glory of God the Father. If we shared in Jesus' death by being baptized, we will be raised to life with him. We know that the persons we used to be were nailed to the cross with Jesus. This was done, so that our sinful bodies would no longer be the slaves of sin."* (Romans 6:3-6 CEV) Just as Jesus died on the cross, was buried, and then rose again, we must do the same. Our baptism is symbolic of the old sinful man dying and the new, clean man being reborn. And, just as Jesus was placed in a tomb, we bury our sinful nature in baptism. What do you do when someone dies? You bury them, and they remain in the grave. The same thing happens with our sin. When we go down into the water, our sins are washed away.

"For we died and were buried with Christ by baptism. And just as Christ was raised from the dead by the glorious power of the Father, now we also may live new lives." **(Romans 6:4 NLT)**

"God is faithful and reliable. If we confess our sins, he forgives them and cleanses us from everything we've done wrong." **(1 John 1:9 GW)**

"By His death, Jesus opened a new and life-giving way through the curtain into the Most Holy Place. And since we have a great High Priest who rules over God's house, let us go right into the presence of God with sincere hearts fully trusting Him. For our guilty consciences have been sprinkled with Christ's blood to make us clean, and our bodies have been washed with pure water." **(Hebrews 10:20-22 NLT)**

---

[6] Webster's II New Riverside Dictionary, pg. 152.

It is a necessary part of salvation, for we must be baptized in order to be saved. (Mark 16:16) Jesus stated plainly that you cannot be saved without baptism. **(Acts 2:38)** On the day of Pentecost, Peter told the Jews that they needed to be baptized.

Baptism is necessary in order to become part of the body of Christ (baptism in Jesus' Name identifies us with others who have done the same). (1 Corinthians 12:13) Whether we have received the Holy Ghost or not, we are not part of the body of Christ until we've been baptized. Without baptism, we will not be an effective part of Christ's church. How can we minister to others if we are not a true part of the body of Christ? You are never too young to minister to others (to minister also means to serve)!

How do we baptize?

If we look at the word Jesus and the apostles used, we find that it means to immerse, submerge, or to make fully wet. (Strong's Greek: baptizo {bap-tid'-zo} 1. to dip repeatedly, to immerse, to submerge; of vessels sunk.[7])

We immerse (or cover completely with water). (Matthew 3:16-17; Acts 8:38; Colossians 2:12) All of these scriptures require a person to be completely immersed, or to go completely under the water. You can't come out of, go down into, or be buried in a few drops of water. When you bury something, you don't just throw a handful of something dirt or sand on it, you cover it completely.

We baptize in the name of Jesus. (Acts 2:38; 8:16; 10:48; 19:5) On the day of Pentecost, Peter commanded us to baptize in the name of Jesus. Throughout the book of Acts, it is recorded that the early church baptized in the name of Jesus. They had just spent 3½ years with Jesus. Having been that close to Him, you would expect that they would know exactly how He would expect them to baptize.

Is baptism necessary?

It was, and is, commanded by Jesus. (Matthew 28:19) *(Teaching note: Do not be concerned about using this scripture. This is an excellent time to briefly discuss the oneness of the Godhead, which will be expounded upon at a later date. God gave the author a personal revelation regarding baptism: even the Trinitarians do not obey their interpretation of this scripture, as they never use a name. They have a good reason. God (or the Father) was called Jehovah (Yahweh) in the Old Testament. In the New Testament, the Son was plainly called Jesus (which means Jehovah-Savior). However, you will find no name that specifically refers to the Holy Ghost. According to their interpretation, they should be baptizing by stating "Jehovah (Yahweh), Jesus, and?" Therein lies their dilemma, as the only name that can be attributed to the Holy Ghost is Jesus. Because they cannot find three names, they simply use words that are plainly not names. In doing this, they disobey the commandment of Jesus to use a name.)*

(Mark 16:15-16) If your Bible has the words of Jesus printed in red, you will notice that this is a commandment given by Jesus Himself. He left no room for a mistake. You must be baptized in order to find salvation.

It was practiced by Jesus and the disciples. (John 4:1-2) Did you know that the disciples baptized others while Jesus was still on the earth?

It was commanded by Peter. (Acts 2:38) Peter was very specific in his command to the Jews at Pentecost. They were told to be baptized *in the name of Jesus*. Peter had just spent 3½ years with Jesus, and there were certainly discussions with Jesus and his disciples about how they should baptize others. There were no disagreements about this among the disciples, for they all baptized in the name of Jesus.

---

[7] Enhanced Strong's Lexicon, (Oak Harbor, WA: Logos Research Systems, Inc.), copyright 1995.

(Acts 10:46-48) The first Gentile (non-Jew) converts were commanded to be baptized in the name of Jesus.

Does it matter how we are baptized?

The disciples of John were required to be re-baptized. (Acts 19:3-6) When Paul met some of John the Baptist's disciples, he directed them to be baptized again in the name of Jesus. It was not enough to simply be baptized, they had to be baptized in Jesus' Name!

This lesson has shown that we must be baptized in Jesus' name to be saved. Let's look at an example that shows why you need to be baptized.

Object lesson: (Time the actions within the object lesson to match what you are teaching.) Put water in the bowl and prepare the doll for "baptism." The children should be able to see that the doll is dirty. While teaching, go through the process of "baptizing" the doll in order to remove the dirt (or "sins"). Additionally, you can dress the doll in the clean clothes in order to signify how our life is changed when we receive the Holy Ghost.

Imagine you have been playing outside all day. It's hot, you are sweaty, and you've been playing in the dirt. Someone inside your house calls out to you and says, "Get cleaned up because you are going to your favorite restaurant!" Excited about going someplace special, you forget about playing outside. You quickly change clothes and say that you are ready to go!

Let's compare this with the "Plan of Salvation." **(Acts 2:38)**

You have repented because you no longer want to play outside. Remember, repentance is simply a change of heart.

You've received the Holy Ghost (you changed your clothes). However, you weren't baptized, because you didn't take a bath! What will your parents' response be? Will it be, "You are not going to the restaurant looking like that? You have dirt all over you!" Will God say, "You're not going to heaven like that? You have sin all over you. You never washed it off!"

Baptism is extremely important. Jesus will not allow someone who has sin in their lives to enter His beautiful, sinless Heaven. We must be baptized in Jesus' name in order to have all of our sins washed away!

THE HOLY GHOST: WHAT IS IT?

Lesson suggestion: Prepare a brightly wrapped gift box for use when explaining the gift of the Holy Ghost.

Hmmm...the Holy Ghost. It sounds sort of scary, doesn't it? I don't especially like ghosts myself. But, the Bible isn't talking about the kind of ghost that some of us have heard about in stories or movies. Just what is the Holy Ghost, why does God want to give it to us, and why is it important that we have it?

Let's look up the definitions of some important words that describe the Holy Ghost.

Holy: Belonging to, derived from, or associated to a divine power.[8]

Divine: Godlike: perfect.[9] How many of us are perfect? We may all know someone who believes that they are perfect: perfect hair, perfect clothes, perfect bedroom, and perfect toys. However, no one is perfect but God. Remember, divine means godlike.

Ghost: The animus: soul [animus is Latin for soul: mind][10]

Spirit: The vital principle or animating force traditionally believed to be within living beings; the Holy Ghost.[11]

The dictionary describes "spirit" as an animating force. What does that mean? Have you ever watched a cartoon? Do you know how they are made? Pictures are drawn, and then put into a video that causes them to move at a fast rate of speed. This makes them actually seem to become alive! If the spirit is an animating force within us, then it is constantly moving and alive inside of us!

If "holy" means Godlike, and a "spirit" is something that is within us, what exactly is the Holy Ghost? It's God's Spirit within us!

Why did God decide to give us the Holy Ghost? God came to earth as a man because He wanted to be with us. He had created man and wanted to be able to spend time with him. After Jesus arose from the tomb, He knew that He would not be able to stay on earth, so He sent down His spirit, called the Holy Ghost (or the Holy Spirit).

"And I will pray the Father, and He shall give you another Comforter, so that He may be with you forever..." **(John 14:16 MKJV)**

"But the Comforter, the Holy Spirit whom the Father will send in My name, He shall teach you all things and bring all things to your remembrance, whatever I have said to you. Peace I leave with you, My peace I give to you. Not as the world gives do I give to you. Let not your heart be troubled, neither let it be afraid." **(John 14:26-27 MKJV)**

Why was the Holy Spirit–or Holy Ghost–called the Comforter? Why do you suppose that God called the Holy Ghost a comforter? When you have the Holy Ghost, it does comfort you! When something comforts you, it makes you feel better!

How many of you have a comforter (or heavy blanket) on your bed? When do you really enjoy your comforter? (Wintertime?) How does your comforter make you feel? (Warm and cozy?) How does the Holy Ghost make you feel? (Encourage feedback: happy, peaceful, full of joy, etc.)

Why wouldn't someone want something that makes them feel so good?

---

[8] Webster's II New Riverside Dictionary, pg. 587.
[9] Webster's II New Riverside Dictionary, pg. 393.
[10] Webster's II New Riverside Dictionary, pg. 529.
[11] Webster's II New Riverside Dictionary, pg. 1121.

DO I NEED THE HOLY GHOST?

Lesson suggestion: Whiteboard, markers. Prepare a brightly wrapped "present" for use in an object lesson.

Last week, we talked about the Holy Ghost and what the Bible says about it. During this lesson, we are going to learn even more about this wonderful gift!

There are so many people that are saying, "All you need to do to be saved is accept Jesus as your personal Savior," or maybe they mention the "Sinner's Prayer." God's salvation requires more of us than just accepting Him, or saying a certain prayer, and this lesson will explain what the Bible says about it.

What is the Holy Ghost? It is a gift from God! The last part of **Acts 2:38** says, *"Ye shall receive the gift of the Holy Ghost."* **(KJV)** In the last lesson, we said that a gift is something given to you that you did not earn. God's gift is something that even the nicest or richest person in the world could not earn. No one deserves this gift, but Jesus offers it to everyone! It doesn't matter how good or bad we have been – Jesus will give it to us, if we simply ask Him for it.

Who is the Holy Ghost? Luke 2:25-32 reminds us of what we learned in the last lesson: the Holy Ghost is the Spirit of God. **Matthew 1:18** tells us that the Holy Ghost was the Father of Jesus. **John 7:37-53** shows that the Holy Ghost was the Spirit of God, and that the Holy Ghost could not be given to man because Jesus had not yet died. In fact, the rulers wanted to arrest Jesus, because they took His words to mean that Jesus was saying that He was God. What we know from these verses is that the Holy Ghost is the Spirit of God.

Do we need the Holy Ghost? Let's look at Peter's response to the question, *"Men and brethren, what shall we do?"* **(Acts 2:38 KJV)** And in **John 3:1-5**, Jesus told Nicodemus, *"Except a man be born again, he cannot see the kingdom of God."* **(KJV)** Jesus was talking about a spiritual birth, which is receiving the Holy Ghost. When Paul met John's disciples, the first question he asked them was, *"Have you received the Holy Ghost since you believed?"* **(Acts 19:1-6 KJV)** Jesus, Peter, and Paul all taught that being filled with the Holy Ghost is necessary for salvation.

How do I know if I've received the Holy Ghost? Let's look at what the apostles say and see what they expected when someone received the Holy Ghost. **Acts 2:4** says that on the day of Pentecost, the disciples spoke with other tongues as the Spirit gave utterance. God gave them the words to say; they did not just make them in their minds. In **Acts 10:44-48**, Peter and those with him were surprised because the Gentiles were speaking in other tongues. The Jews were amazed that God was pouring out His Spirit on the Gentiles by filling them with the Holy Ghost. **Acts 1:8** talks about another sign that one should expect when they receive the Holy Ghost: power! The Holy Ghost gives us power to overcome sin!

When we have repented (changed our hearts and direction), been baptized in the name of Jesus, and have received the Holy Ghost (God living in us), we have the ability to build a relationship with Him. And, through that relationship, we have the privilege to expect that when we pray to Him, He will hear and answer our prayers.

Now that we've decided that the Holy Ghost is a good thing, how do we get it? What exactly must we do to receive it? **Have the children quote Acts 2:38**: *"Then Peter said unto them, Repent, and be baptized every one of you in the name of Jesus Christ for the remission of sins, and ye shall receive the gift of the Holy Ghost."* **(KJV)**

We have already studied repentance, so most of us should already know what it means to repent. Can anyone tell me? (To make a change, etc.) We feel bad about things we've done, and we want to change and not do them anymore!

First, we must repent and ask Him to forgive us for the bad things that we have done. To repent means to feel such regret for previous behavior as to change one's mind about it[12]. Repentance is not just asking for forgiveness, it is deciding to make a change in our actions! Once we've asked Jesus to clean out our heart, He can move in; God can't live in a dirty heart!

Next, we need to be baptized. How? (In the name of Jesus Christ) Why? To remove our sins! **(Acts 2:38; 19:5)** And, you will receive the gift of the Holy Ghost! Did you know that you can get the Holy Ghost before you're baptized, too? God isn't going to tell you that you have to wait!

Wait! What did the end of that verse say? *"...and ye shall receive the **gift** of the Holy Ghost."*

What does "the Holy Ghost is a gift" mean? The dictionary says that a gift is something that a person gives to you without asking for payment!

Object lesson: Use a brightly wrapped gift box. Invite a child up to receive the gift; however, as they reach to receive their present, place stipulations upon them. (e.g., vacuum the classroom, pick up paper around the church, stack the chairs, etc.) "Once you've finished those things for me, I'll give you this present."

"Now, was I really giving them a gift? No! They had to work in return for receiving it!"

We don't receive gifts because we earn them, but because people love us and want to give us something special! That's the way it is with the Holy Ghost! We haven't done anything to earn the Holy Ghost; God simply wants us to have it!

What happens when you are praying and asking God for the Holy Ghost, and He starts to move into your heart? God created all of us with a mind. It is the action center where our thoughts and decisions take place. So, when you are praying for the Holy Ghost and God begins to give it to you, you will start to hear words in your mind. The words probably won't make sense to you, because God will not have you speak a language that you already know. You will know when He speaks in your mind, because it won't sound like you! It is important that you decide to listen to His voice, and then, you must say the words that you hear (in your mind) out loud.

Our tongue is the hardest thing for us to control, so it's the part of us that God chooses to take control of when He fills us with the Holy Ghost. It is important that you choose to let Him move your tongue around. If you keep forcing yourself to speak words that you already know, you will not receive the Holy Ghost, because He has to have control of your tongue in order to fill you with His Spirit!

Your lips might start to feel really funny, sort of like how they quiver after you've been outside in the cold. Your tongue will start moving in a funny way, and you'll hear yourself say words you've never spoken before! **Isaiah 28:11** says, *"For with stammering lips and another tongue He will speak to this people."* **(KJV)**

When someone starts speaking in their Holy Ghost language, it might sound like baby talk. Have you ever heard a baby speak? They start out by making sounds like "Ga-ga" or "Goo-goo." Their first word might be "Mama," or "Dada." A baby's first words will never sound like a grown-up's. That is how it is with the Holy Ghost, too. When you first begin speaking in a heavenly language, it will probably sound like Holy Ghost baby talk. That is okay; say those words! It's not possible to say them incorrectly!

(Acts 2:4, 38) God gives you a new language because He wants you to have evidence (or proof) that He is moving into your heart! **(Acts 19:6)**

---

[12] Webster's II New Riverside Dictionary, pg. 996.

Once you have received the Holy Ghost, you will feel different emotions. Many people feel love and joy, because when Jesus moves into a heart, He is there to stay, and it feels so good! Once God gives the Holy Ghost to someone, they are never alone again. **Hebrews 13:5** says, *"For he hath said, I will never leave thee, nor forsake thee."* **(KJV)** Anyone who has received the Holy Ghost (or Holy Spirit) has a BFF (Best Friend Forever): Jesus!

(Isaiah 12:3; Habakkuk 3:18; Acts 13:52; Romans 14:17; 15:13; Galatians 5:22-23)

(At the close of this lesson, we suggest taking time for prayer. You may have children in your group who are moved by this lesson and want to pray for the Holy Ghost.)

HOW SOFT IS YOUR DIRT?

Lesson suggestion: *Collect soil samples of both hard and soft dirt (there are four different types of soil mentioned in the parable of the sower). Our focus is on whether our students' "heart soil" is hard or soft; a "seed bag" (something that would demonstrate what a sower would use), or a package of seeds.*

I have a question. It may sound silly to you, but you'll understand why I ask it after we finish this lesson. *"How soft is your dirt?"* The scripture that we're about to read will help you understand my question. Let's read from the Bible: **(Mark 4:3-8 CEV)** *"Now listen! A farmer went out to scatter seed in a field. While the farmer was scattering the seed, some of it fell along the road and was eaten by birds. Other seeds fell on thin, rocky ground and quickly started growing because the soil wasn't very deep. But when the sun came up, the plants were scorched and dried up, because they did not have enough roots. Some other seeds fell where thornbushes grew up and choked out the plants. So they did not produce any grain. But a few seeds did fall on good ground where the plants grew and produced thirty or sixty or even a hundred times as much as was scattered."*

This scripture talks about a farmer who was getting ready for his next crop. For our lesson, we will call him Farmer Brown. Unfortunately, in Bible days they didn't have any big and fancy farm tractors available for Farmer Brown to use. *Back then, the farmers were called sowers because they had to "sow" their own seed (to "sow" means to "scatter seed").* So, Farmer Brown prepared his seed and planned for a nice long day out in the hot sun. He probably packed a good-sized lunch to take along. After all, he would not be returning home for a while! The Bible doesn't say how big the farmer's field was, but it was probably a very big one! He probably had to take quite a bit of seed along with him for the job.

When he got to the field, Farmer Brown set down his lunch and puts the bag of seed over his shoulder. It must have been so heavy! He walked to the farthest point of his field, dipped his hand into the bag, and grabbed a handful of seed; then, he began to throw it about. The ground had just been ploughed, but there was no way he could be sure that all of the dirt was fertile (or good) soil. He was just hoping that the seeds would end up in a good spot where they will grow! Here's what happened:

Hard Dirt

(Mark 4:4 CEV) *"...some of it fell along the road and was eaten by birds."* "Along the road" is also called the way side; it would be hard, like a path that many people had walked upon. The farmer hadn't ploughed this part of the field at all!

(Mark 4:15 CEV) *"The seeds that fell along the road are the people who hear the message. But Satan soon comes and snatches it away from them."* The hearts of some people are very hard, just like a sidewalk made out of concrete. No matter how much they hear God's Word, it can never sink below the surface. They are so involved with sin that it cannot take root.

Shallow Dirt

(Mark 4:5-6 CEV) *"Other seeds fell on thin, rocky ground and quickly started growing because the soil wasn't very deep. But when the sun came up, the plants were scorched and dried up, because they did not have enough roots."* The seeds found a home, but the dirt was very shallow and there were rocks underneath it. Once the plants' roots were long enough to reach the rocks, they died because they could not pass through.

(Mark 4:16-17 CEV) *"The seeds that fell on rocky ground are the people who gladly hear the message and accept it right away. But they don't have any roots, and they don't last very long. As soon as life gets hard or the message gets them in trouble, they give up."* These hearts are a little softer. The people love to hear God's Word but sadly, they are not changed by it. They are most likely the person that goes to church every Sunday and worships like they should. However, when Monday morning arrives, their life seems to fall apart. Problems come, things go wrong, and they just can't handle it. We call these people "Shallow Christians."

Thorny Dirt

(Mark 4:7 CEV) *"Some other seeds fell where thornbushes grew up and choked out the plants. So they did not produce any grain."* The earth had been ploughed, but no one had ever removed the weeds and thorns from it. When the seeds began to grow, the new plants became entangled in the thorn bushes and weeds. Eventually, all of the plants simply died.

(Mark 4:18-19 CEV) *"The seeds that fell among the thornbushes are also people who hear the message. But they start worrying about the needs of this life. They are fooled by the desire to get rich and to have all kinds of other things. So the message gets choked out, and they never produce anything."* These people, like the "Shallow Christian," have heard and accepted God's Word. It has even rooted a little bit deeper. Unfortunately, they don't let God have full control of their life. They don't work at having a daily relationship with Him. They don't develop the habit of praying and reading their Bible every day. The worries of life control them, and sin (like a thorn bush) is able to creep back into their life. As sin gains control, the Word of God is crowded out. This is what we call "backsliding." A backslider is one who turns from obedience to God and falls into sin. We call it backsliding simply because instead of growing their relationship with God, they are going backwards instead. Instead of living for God, they have chosen to focus on themselves.

Good Dirt

(Mark 4:8 CEV) *"But a few seeds did fall on good ground where the plants grew and produced thirty or sixty or even a hundred times as much as was scattered."* A farmer loves this type of ground! The plough did a great job in this part of the field; the weeds and other bad things had been taken away, and the good ground was very fertile! All of the minerals and other things that the plants needed in order to grow existed there, so every plant grew to be tall and healthy.

(Mark 4:20 CEV) *"The seeds that fell on good ground are the people who hear and welcome the message. They produce thirty or sixty or even a hundred times as much as was planted."* The good ground was fruitful! The dictionary defines "fruitful" as *"very productive; producing fruit in abundance; as fruitful soil."*[13] This means that people with fruitful hearts not only serve God and have a relationship with Him, they are also witnesses for Him! They teach Home Bible Studies; they are an example at work and at school; they let God's light shine through them every day. As a result, *many* other people come to know about God's love. This is what is meant by producing thirty, or sixty, or even a hundred times more than what was planted.

Our sower, Farmer Brown, is like Jesus. "How?" you ask. He was a sower of spiritual seeds! Jesus taught many people about the love of God. He did miracles and wonderful things that showed everyone who He really was: God in a human body. Sadly, not everyone believed the message He taught.

Like Farmer Brown, your pastor is also a sower! He sows spiritual seed by preaching the Word of God to you. Even more seed is sown when he teaches Bible Study and tells the church important things that they must know. However, just like in the Bible days, not everyone listens and allows God to change them.

---

[13] Noah Webster's 1828 Dictionary of American English

Do you remember the question I asked you at the beginning of this lesson? *"How soft is your dirt?"* Is it like the hard, shallow, or thorny dirt in our lesson? Or, is it like "good dirt," ready for Jesus to plant His love there so it will grow?

I'm going to read a few verses, and then I would like us to take just a few minutes to talk to Jesus.

- **(Psalm 51:10-12 CEV)** *"Create pure thoughts in me and make me faithful again."*
- **(Psalm 139:23-24 KJV)** *"Search me, O God, and know my heart: try me, and know my thoughts: And see if there be any wicked way in me, and lead me in the way everlasting."*
- **Psalm 51:11-12 CEV)** *"Don't chase me away from you or take your Holy Spirit away from me. Make me as happy as you did when you saved me; make me want to obey!"*
- **(Psalm 119:10 CEV)** *"I worship you with all my heart. Don't let me walk away from your commands."*

I want the "dirt" of my heart to be soft so that I can be fruitful for Him, don't you? Repentance is something that we must do every day. It keeps our heart in a soft condition so that He can change us into what we need to be. Let's ask Him to clean our hearts out right now!

BEING CONSISTENT IN ALL THINGS

Lesson suggestion: Whiteboard, markers.

We will do many things throughout our lives. *(Teacher: give a short 'progressive' picture of how your life has evolved from childhood to adulthood.)* We all have to attend school from Kindergarten to graduation. Many of you will go on to college, and most of you will get married. Others will go into the military, and many will begin working at a job. In spite of the differences in all of these things, they will all require one thing: *consistency*. Right now, you have kid-type things to do. You still have at least six more years of school left, and some of you have a whole lot more! You have rooms to clean, chores to do, tests to take, and friends to make! You have memory verses to learn, a Bible to read, and prayer time to complete each day. You have an attitude to keep track of and actions to watch constantly.

To be consistent means to be *"fixed; firm; not fluid; as the consistent parts of a body."*[14] Does your body change shape? No, it doesn't, except when you get taller and gain or lose weight! Your arms and legs don't switch places! What are some areas in which we need to be consistent? *(Ask for student feedback)*

How can we be consistent in friendships? How should we treat others on a regular basis?

- Love them at all times, regardless of circumstance.
- Show God's love and help others with their problems.
  (Proverbs 17:17; 18:24; 27:17)

How can we be consistent in our schooling? What must we do to pass all of our tests, to make sure our homework is done?

- Study on a regular basis.
- Finish all of our homework before playing.

Think about this: A flower garden will never grow unless it is either consistently watered, or it consistently rains. Or, a pattern will not be correct if the shapes are not consistent *(draw both a consistent and inconsistent pattern on the board)*.

How can we be consistent in our relationship with God?

- Read our Bible every day.
- Have a consistent, daily prayer habit (although it's not required, it helps if it occurs at the same time).
- Talk to others about Jesus.
- Resist the temptation to do things that we shouldn't; rely on God when we get in trouble. **(1 Peter 5:8)**
- Make up our mind that no matter what happens, we are going to live for Jesus.
  (1 Corinthians 15:58)

Here are some more things to think about. A baby that is not consistently shown affection, by receiving hugs or kisses from its mom and dad, will not truly learn the meaning of love. A dog that is consistently beaten or kicked will learn to fear and then, retaliate (or fight back) in self-defense. A friend that you treat badly will no longer trust that he or she is really your friend.

---

[14] Noah Webster's 1828 Dictionary of American English

Here are some even *bigger* things to think about:

- *If you consistently wait for others to lead, you will never be a leader.*
- *If you consistently wait for your friends (or your family) to begin living for God before you do, you will most likely never live for Him.*
- *If you consistently wait to be told when to pray, you will most likely never pray on your own.*
- *If you consistently wait to be told when to read your Bible, rather than do it on your own, you will most likely never read it.*

Wow. Let's think about that for a minute. *We* decide how successful, or unsuccessful, we're going to be in every area of our lives!

The greatest example that we have of consistency is in Jesus Himself. No matter what came His way, He *never* changed, and Jesus went through some pretty hard things in His lifetime! The Bible does not say that living for God will be easy. We have learned before that the devil is very consistent, because he continually tries to get you to mess up!

There's a scripture in the Bible that talks about the example that Jesus left for us to follow. Let's read about it: **(1 Peter 2:21-24 NLT)** *"This suffering is all part of what God has called you to. Christ, who suffered for you, is your example. Follow in his steps. He never sinned, and he never deceived anyone. He did not retaliate when he was insulted. When he suffered, he did not threaten to get even. He left his case in the hands of God, who always judges fairly. He personally carried away our sins in his own body on the cross so we can be dead to sin and live for what is right. You have been healed by his wounds!"* **(John 13:12-16; 1 Timothy 4:12)**

Let's pray and ask Jesus to help us be consistent in our relationship with Him. He *will* help us. We only have to ask Him!

HOW CAN I GAIN FORGIVENESS?

Lesson suggestion: Whiteboard, markers.

The Bible says that all have sinned. **Romans 3:23** says, *"Because all people have sinned, they have fallen short of God's glory."* **(GW)** If we have all sinned, and sin causes death, how can we escape this punishment? If God will not allow sin to enter into heaven, how can we ever hope to go to there? **(Revelation 20:11-15)** This is where forgiveness comes on the scene. Because we have sinned, we need to find forgiveness.

What is forgiveness?

The Bible says that we need forgiveness, so it is very important that we understand it. When the scriptures speak of forgiveness, they are referring to a person having received a pardon, or a removal of a punishment. Just think about what that means! Once we receive forgiveness for our sins, we will not get the punishment that we deserve!

Let's look at what the Bible says about forgiveness. First, we will begin in the Old Testament. God required sacrifices for someone to obtain forgiveness for any sins that they had committed. Additionally, **Numbers 15:27** and **Leviticus 5:17-19** both talk about a person's need to offer a sacrifice for unknown sins. This means that they didn't know whether or not they had committed a sin; they just had to make sure they were forgiven. Can you imagine living under those rules? Most of us would need to offer a sacrifice every day, just so we could be sure that God was still pleased with us!

(Numbers 15:27 GW) *"If one person unintentionally does something wrong, a one-year-old female goat must be sacrificed as an offering for sin."*

(Leviticus 5:17-19 GW) *"If any of you do wrong--even one thing forbidden by any of the LORD's commands, but you didn't know it--when you realize your guilt, you must be punished. You must bring the priest a ram that has no defects from the flock or its value in money for a guilt offering. The priest will make peace with the LORD for the wrong you did unintentionally (although you didn't know what you did), and you will be forgiven. It is a guilt offering because you are certainly guilty as far as the LORD is concerned."*

God realized that this law placed a large burden on man, so He decided that He would remove the need for us to offer sacrifices at all! God did this by coming to earth as a baby named Jesus; then, Jesus offered Himself as the ultimate sacrifice for our sin when He was crucified on the cross. The verses found in **Hebrews 9:22, 28** explain that the law of God required a blood sacrifice of some kind, because without blood there was no forgiveness. In the Old Testament, God had required the sacrifice of a spotless, unblemished, and perfect animal (this meant that there could be absolutely no markings on the animal, and it had to be completely healthy; there could be nothing wrong with it at all). In the New Testament, Jesus Christ was offered as the sacrifice, or payment, for our sins. Following His death on the cross, Jesus came to life again after three days. We will be learning more about this later on!

Let's look at the verse we use the most to tell how to be saved: **Acts 2:38**. Does this verse say anything about forgiveness? Yes! If you read it in the NIV translation, you will see that it uses the word "forgiveness" in place of "remission." These two words have the same meaning.

How do we obtain (or get) forgiveness?

We've already discussed how Jesus died for our sins, but how do we take advantage of His death? It is plainly stated in Acts 2:38 that we need to repent! Remember, that's a change of heart, or a change of direction. We turn away from sin and go towards God. We need to be baptized in the name of Jesus. If you have not performed both of these steps, your sins have not been forgiven.

You may say, "I've already done that, but I've sinned again. Do I need to repent and be baptized again?" Yes, you need to repent and make a decision to change. No, you do not need to be baptized each time that you sin! Let's look at **1 John 1:9**. This verse tells us that we need to confess (or admit) our sins to Him; then, God will forgive us. You simply need to go to Jesus, tell Him what you did, and that you will change.

Now you may ask, "How do I know that He will forgive me?" The Bible also has an answer for that question. **Luke 5:18-26** tells about a sick man who simply wanted to be healed. Did you notice that Jesus didn't even tell him that he was healed? He simply told the man that his sins were forgiven! Jesus loved this man so much that He not only healed him, He also forgave his sins; the man hadn't even asked to be forgiven! **Matthew 9:2** and **Mark 2:5** also give examples of times that Jesus, when asked to heal someone, also forgave sins at the same time without even being asked. That should tell you how important forgiveness is to Jesus, and just how eager He is to forgive our sins!

Have you ever wondered, "How many times will Jesus forgive me?" Will He ever decide to stop offering forgiveness for sins? **In Matthew 18:21-22**, Jesus tells his disciples to forgive the same wrong at least 490 times. Would Jesus require less of Himself that he would us? No! God always requires more of Himself than He does of us. While this doesn't give us permission to sin, it does allow us to come to God with confidence that, when we need to ask His forgiveness, He will be ready to forgive us for what we have done wrong.

Is there anything that can keep us from receiving God's forgiveness? Actually, there is: a lack of forgiveness. **Mark 11:25-26** tells us that if we do not forgive others, Jesus will not forgive us. This is why it is so important not to hold a grudge against someone, or to stay mad at them. What if you would die before you forgave them? You cannot go to heaven with bitterness against someone in your heart. **(Hebrews 12:15 KJV)** *"Make sure that everyone has kindness from God so that bitterness doesn't take root and grow up to cause trouble that corrupts many of you."* Is there something you need to resolve so that you can obtain forgiveness? If there is anyone that you need to forgive, ask Jesus to help you. He will be happy to help you forgive them, because He wants nothing more than to extend His forgiveness to us. We simply need to ask Him!

"TO-DO LIST" PRIORITY #1:
Work on My Relationship with God

Lesson suggestion: Whiteboard, markers.

Today's lesson deals with the different types of relationships that we have all experienced at one time or another. Most importantly, we're going to talk about our relationship with God. The dictionary says that a relationship is *"the state of being related by kindred, affinity or other alliance."*[15] Now, the dictionary always uses *really* big words, so we're going to break this definition down so that you can understand it better! Let's write these on the board as we go. That way, we can refer back to the words throughout the lesson.

When you have a *"relationship by kindred,"* it means you are related to someone *by birth* (parents, sister, or brother); or, to be related to someone *by marriage* (husband, wife, mother-in-law, father-in-law, your husband or wife's brothers and sisters, called brothers-in-law or sisters-in-law); or, *by affinity*. Affinity is kind of funny word, isn't it? It means *to agree or resemble.* So, how would you have a *relationship by affinity*? Let's think about this. When you think about your best friend, what comes to mind? Do you both enjoy the same things, *or are you opposites*? It would be difficult to be best friends with someone who did not enjoy the things that you do. What would you talk about? How would you have fun playing together, if you didn't enjoy the same types of toys or games? What about eating a snack together? You'd never be able to decide what kind of food to share! So having a *relationship of affinity* is *to have a relationship, or friendship, with someone that has the same interests as you!*

Now that we understand the different types of relationships that we can have, let's talk about the ones that we have right now. I'll start! I am a *(father/mother)*; I am a *(brother/sister)*; I am a *(husband/wife)*. I am also a teacher, which means that *we* have a relationship! I am also a friend, because I have a friendship with _____ *(teacher, talk about a special friend).*

I have another big word that we need to learn! *Cultivate.* C-U-L-T-I-V-A-T-E. Let's all say it together! So, what does the dictionary say about the word "cultivate?" *"To improve by labor or study; to advance the growth of."*[16] How does this word apply to our relationships? We must cultivate them! We must study them in order to figure out what we need to add or take away from them. We need to make our relationships grow!

Does a plant grow without water? No! Does a baby learn to talk if it is not taught? No! Does a dog learn to roll over on command all by itself? No! Just as these things won't grow without help, our relationships will not grow if we don't work on them.

The relationship with our parents or guardian is very important. They are the ones to whom God has given the responsibility of raising us up to be good people and good Christians **(Deuteronomy 6:5-7)**. It is also *our* responsibility to obey and respect their God-given job. **(Ephesians 6:1 KJV)** *"Children, obey your parents in the Lord: for this is right."* We must communicate with either our parents or the one that takes care of us. We need to tell them our hurts and disappointments, about what makes us happy or sad. We need to tell them about our days at school, and our lessons in Sunday School! We need to tell them about our field trip to the zoo, or about the cool dog we saw while we were outside riding our bikes. We need to ask them questions when we don't understand something, or when we are confused. We also need to ask them about *their* day, and hug them when they're sad. We need to dry their tears when they feel bad, and fix them hot tea or soup when they feel sick! All of these things are important because each one builds upon that relationship. If you don't spend time with someone, you won't know anything about them, and they won't know anything about you. That is not a relationship!

---

[15] Noah Webster's 1828 Dictionary of American English
[16] Noah Webster's 1828 Dictionary of American English

Now! We've learned about the different kinds of relationships that we can have with other people. What about our relationship with God? What types of relationships do we have, or can we have, with Him?

- **Father:** *"Let your light so shine before men, that they may see your good works, and glorify your Father which is in heaven."* **(Matthew 5:16 KJV)**
- **Friend:** *"A man that hath friends must show himself friendly: and there is a friend that sticketh closer than a brother."* **(Proverbs 18:24 KJV)**
- **Counselor:** *"For unto us a child is born, unto us a son is given: and the government shall be upon his shoulder: and his name shall be called Wonderful, Counselor, The mighty God, The everlasting Father, The Prince of Peace."* (A counselor is someone who gives advice.) **(Isaiah 9:6 KJV)**
- **Teacher:** *"The same came to Jesus by night, and said unto him, Rabbi, we know that thou art a teacher come from God: for no man can do these miracles that thou doest, except God be with him."* **(John 3:2 KJV)**

We've listed four things that God can be to us. The Bible says He is our Father, Friend, Counselor, and Teacher. But how can we cultivate (or grow) our relationship with God so that He can fill all of these roles in our life every day? *(Class feedback)* We've talked about these two things many times. That's right; we must pray and read God's Word! Now, prayer is really just a fancy word that means talking to God. We talk to people every day! We talk to our parents, friends, teachers, the woman at the grocery store, the neighbor next door, the man at the gas station, and even our animals! What could be so hard about talking to God? Nothing! It's not hard at all! Actually, it's easier to talk to Him than others sometimes, because He'll never laugh at anything you say. He'll never say anything back to you that will make you feel bad. He won't tell you to be quiet, or that He is busy and doesn't have time for you. He won't make you feel like you're not important. He loves you! He *wants* you to talk to Him. When you think about what I've just said, *why* wouldn't *you want to talk to Him*? I can't think of one reason not to!

There is an awesome thing that happens when we make a habit out of talking to God every day. He begins to talk back to us! Really, He does! Now, it doesn't sound like my voice does right now. It is a still, quiet voice in your mind. **(1 Kings 19:11, 12)** It has a distinct sound, and when He speaks to you, your Holy Ghost will recognize His voice. However, it is important to remember that God's voice is quiet. If you are always talking and are never listening, you will not be able to hear Him talk to you. You must practice being quiet.

Revelation 3:20 says, *"Look! Here I stand at the door and knock. If you hear me calling and open the door, I will come in, and we will share a meal as friends."* **(NLT)** Jesus is waiting to talk to you; what are you waiting for?

PRAYER, LESSON #1
Developing our Relationship with God

Lesson suggestion: Whiteboard, markers. As there are a number of scriptures included in this lesson, we suggest handing out "reading assignments" prior to class so that the children can assist you with the lesson. They will enjoy it!

What is prayer?

To **"pray"** means to humbly make a request, to address God with love and adoration, repentance, supplication, or thanksgiving. *To make this easier for you to understand, prayer is simply talking with God, our friend.*

Prayer is our chance to talk to God.

What types of relationships can we have with Him? (Father, friend, teacher, etc.) Think of similar relationships we have with people. Do those relationships require talking? How can we truly have a relationship with someone if we don't talk with them?

Prayer is our chance to learn about God.

How do you learn about someone, like a new friend? How would you learn more about God? *(Class participation)*

Prayer helps us live an overcoming life (which means we will be able to conquer our problems with God's help). There are hundreds of verses in the Bible that talk about someone praying when they were sick, sad, in trouble, lost, about to die, and more. And, the Bible tells how God answered their prayers!

What if I don't pray?

You won't have a relationship with God, and you won't have any power against sin when Satan tempts you!

Are there different ways to pray?

    Praise: **Psalms 34:1-2; 150:1-6**
    Worship: **Matthew 4:10; John 4:24**
    Thanksgiving: **Psalm 100:1-5; Philippians 4:6**
    Intercession: **Romans 8:26-34; Ephesians 6:17-20**

When should I pray?

Both before *and* after you receive the Holy Ghost! **(Luke 21:36; Acts 10:1-6; 1 Thessalonians 5:17)**

Where should I pray?

We can pray at any time and in any place. It doesn't matter where you are or what you are doing. Jesus is always ready to listen to us!

But it's so hard to pray. How do I make it easier?

Let's think about this for a minute. What would make it hard for us to pray? What things can we do to make it easier?

- Are we are trying to hide something from God? **(Proverbs 15:29)**

- Practice makes perfect, so we should work to create a habit! **(Acts 3:1; Psalm 63:1; Daniel 6:10)**
- We can choose a prayer project (ex: lost friend or family member). Having something specific to pray for helps keep our focus in the proper place!

Start with short prayer times and grow (5 min, 10 min, 15 min). *(Teacher, we suggest that each child begin by praying an amount of time equivalent to their age. For some, that may be too long. A child who has never prayed can begin with a few minutes and work their way up. God will be pleased, whatever the effort, when they are working to grow in Him.)*

Give God a chance to talk to you, too! If you are doing all the talking, you can't hear what He may be trying to say to you. The more time you spend with Him, the easier it is to hear Him speak. *(Teacher note: There are many scriptures that detail how God spoke to the prophets of Israel. A suggestion would be to use one of those scriptures as an example of how God, when answering a prophet's prayer, would tell them what say to the Israelite people.)*

PRAYER, LESSON #2
Developing our Relationship with God

Lesson suggestion: Whiteboard, markers. A 21-day-habit chart, along with guidelines for use, can be found in the Teacher's Toolbox at the back of this book.

Have you ever noticed that there are times when it is hard to pray? You really do try, but you just run out of things to say after about 5 minutes. We know that we should pray, but we just can't seem to do it very well. The word definition of "pray" has changed over time. When the Bible was translated to English, it was a very common word. There are older words that could have also replaced the word "*pray*" back when the Bible was being translated into different languages (to "translate" means to interpret or explain): *seek, ask, desire, request, beg, talk, complain, speak, want, long for, intercede, consult, praise, wish, cry out, comfort, encourage, and instruct.*

Here is an example of how "pray" was used back in earlier times: *"I pray thee, see that everyone has a Bible for class."* Did I pray and ask God to help everyone remember to bring their Bible? No, I just asked you to make sure that everyone had a Bible to use. The English language has changed quite a lot over time!

Just what is prayer? Let's look at what we call *The Lord's Prayer*, found in **Matthew 6:9-15**. Our best example in prayer is Jesus. Let's focus on a few things concerning this instruction given by Jesus.

Prayer should be sincere.

We do not pray so that others will recognize us, we pray because we want to spend time with God. **(Matthew 6:5)**

Prayer should be a consistent, regular habit.

Jesus said, *"When"* you pray, not *"if"* you pray. He expects that if He is truly our friend, we will *want* to talk to Him. **(Daniel 6:10)**

Prayer should not simply be vain repetitions (saying the same thing over and over again). **See Matthew 6:7.**

Here is an example that may surprise you. During yoga exercises, you may see someone sitting on the floor with their legs crossed; they may also be holding their forefinger and thumb in a circle. This is actually a part of Hindu worship, and part of a Hindu's prayer-time can be to sit that way and say "Aum" over and over. Did you know that "Aum" is the name of a Hindu god? We need to make sure that we understand why people do strange or interesting things sometimes; we don't want to pray to an idol without even knowing that we're doing it! It's also important to know that simply repeating a word or phrase over and over will not help us!

Prayer is necessary.

Jesus knows what we need before we ask Him for it, but He will often wait until we ask before He gives it to us. **(Matthew 6:8b)**

Prayer should always begin with thanksgiving, praise, and worship.

In fact, this should be a major part of our prayer. **(Psalm 22:3)**

Forgiveness is essential to prayer.

Have you ever held a grudge toward someone? (A grudge can happen when we feel anger towards someone about a specific thing.) Do you want Jesus to hold a grudge against you? Jesus said that if we do not forgive others, He will not forgive us. We should *always* be ready to forgive others, even when it is not an easy thing to do; our salvation depends upon it. **(Matthew 18:21-22; Mark 11:25-26)**

You may say, "I'm just a child. My prayers aren't important. I can't even pray a long time. Do you know how important you are to God? Let's look in the Bible! **1 Samuel 3:1-10** tells about how Samuel was chosen by God to lead Israel when he was a child. Jeremiah was scolded for thinking that his age would keep him from doing what God told him to do. **(Jeremiah 1:1-10)** Jesus talked about children often. And, in **Mark 10:13-16**, when his disciples were trying to protect Him for being bothered by children, Jesus told them to encourage the little ones to come to Him. Jesus even let the children sit upon His knee while He talked to the adults!

How do we develop a relationship with God? You may say, "I already pray at meals and at bedtime. Isn't that enough?" That is a great way to start! However, this lesson is encouraging us to take another step in our relationship with Jesus.

Did you know that if you do something for 3 weeks, you will have created a new habit? We are going to learn a little more about prayer, and then we will spend 21 days developing our habit of talking with Jesus!

THE EIGHT AREAS OF PRAYER:
Introduction to the Prayer Wheel

Lesson suggestion: *A Prayer Wheel pattern and "instructions for use" are located in the Teacher's Toolbox. It is advantageous to have a prayer wheel available for every child's use. Plan to have the children practice as you teach the lesson, as it will help them understand how to apply each part to their individual prayer time.*

How many of you like to talk to Jesus? We're going to introduce a new prayer tool in this lesson: the prayer wheel. We have made one especially for you! There are eight "pie slices" on the wheel, and each one focuses on a different way to communicate with God.

Tell God He is great and He does great work (Praise and Worship)

The Bible contains many verses that talk about praise and worship. God is mighty! He is everlasting!

- **(1 Chronicles 16:29 KJV)** *"Give unto the LORD the glory due unto his name: bring an offering, and come before him: worship the LORD in the beauty of holiness."*
- **(Psalm 86:9 KJV)** *"All nations whom thou hast made shall come and worship before thee, O Lord; and shall glorify thy name."*
- **(Psalm 99:5 KJV)** *"Exalt ye the LORD our God, and worship at his footstool; for he is holy."*
- **(Psalm 145:10 GNT)** *"All your creatures, LORD, will praise you, and all your people will give you thanks."*

Ask for a clean heart (Repentance)

It is important that we ask God to clean the bad things out of our heart every day. Repenting just one time does not cover everything that we do wrong in God's sight. We must search our heart every day; this helps us make sure that there is nothing there that displeases Him.

- **(Ezekiel 18:30b GW)** *"Change the way you think and act. Turn away from all the rebellious things that you have done so that you will not fall into sin."*
- **(Luke 13:3 KJV)** *"I tell you, Nay: but, except ye repent, ye shall all likewise perish."*
- **(Acts 3:19 KJV)** *"Repent ye therefore, and be converted, that your sins may be blotted out, when the times of refreshing shall come from the presence of the Lord..."*
- **(Revelation 3:19 GW)** *"I correct and discipline everyone I love. Take this seriously, and change the way you think and act."*

Tell God my needs (Petitions; requests)

God has promised that He would supply everything that we need. He also said that He would not put more trouble on us than we can handle! Do you have something that is really bothering you? You can tell God all about it. Because He is God, Jesus loves us more than anyone else possibly could!

- **(Matthew 6:8b CEV)** *"Your Father knows what you need before you ask."*
- **(Philippians 4:19 KJV)** *"But my God shall supply all your need according to his riches in glory by Christ Jesus."*
- **(Hebrews 4:16 CEV)** *"So whenever we are in need, we should come bravely before the throne of our merciful God. There we will be treated with undeserved kindness, and we will find help."*
- **(Isaiah 53:5 KJV)** *"But he was wounded for our transgressions, he was bruised for our iniquities: the chastisement of our peace was upon him; and with his stripes we are healed."*

Pray for Others (Intercession)

There are many different ways to pray for others. Here are just a few:

- **Healing: (James 5:15a KJV)** *"And the prayer of faith shall save the sick, and the Lord shall raise him up..."*
- **Salvation: (Luke 15:7 GW)** *"I can guarantee that there will be more happiness in heaven over one person who turns to God and changes the way he thinks and acts than over 99 people who already have turned to God and have his approval."*
- **Unkindness: (Matthew 5:44 CEV)** *"But I tell you to love your enemies and pray for anyone who mistreats you."*
- **Soul-winners: (Luke 10:2 GW)** *"He told them, "The harvest is large, but the workers are few. So ask the Lord who gives this harvest to send workers to harvest his crops."*
- **Faithfulness: (Hebrews 13:18 KJV)** *"Pray for us: for we trust we have a good conscience, in all things willing to live honestly."*

Thank God for all the good things He has done (Thanksgiving)

God does great things for all of us. Just think about this for a minute! What has He done for you? (Provided a place to live, food to eat, etc.) We are all here together because He let us live to see another day! What has God done for you? *(Ask for a few short "popcorn" testimonies.)*

- **(1 Chronicles 16:34 KJV)** *"O give thanks unto the LORD; for he is good; for his mercy endureth forever."*
- **(Psalms 106:2 CEV)** *"No one can praise you enough for all of the mighty things you have done."*
- **(Psalms 145:4 KJV)** *"One generation shall praise thy works to another, and shall declare thy mighty acts."*
- **(Psalm 139:14, KJV)** *"I will praise thee; for I am fearfully and wonderfully made: marvelous are thy works; and that my soul knoweth right well."*

Think about God and listen for His voice (Meditation)

God would love nothing more than for us to sit and listen for Him to talk to us. Many times, we are so busy telling Him about our problems that we forget to just "be quiet" in His presence!

- **(Job 37:2 KJV)** *"Hear attentively the noise of his voice, and the sound that goeth out of his mouth."*
- **(1 Kings 19:11-12 KJV)** *"And he said, Go forth, and stand upon the mount before the LORD. And, behold, the LORD passed by, and a great and strong wind rent the mountains, and broke in pieces the rocks before the LORD; but the LORD was not in the wind: and after the wind an earthquake; but the LORD was not in the earthquake: And after the earthquake a fire; but the LORD was not in the fire: and after the fire <u>a still small voice</u>."* (additional formatting by author)
- **(John 10:3b-4 KJV)** *"...the sheep hear his voice: and he calleth his own sheep by name, and leadeth them out. And when he putteth forth his own sheep, he goeth before them, and the sheep follow him: for they know his voice."*

Pray God's Word

Praying God's Word is very simple. We just need to open our Bible and choose a scripture to read aloud during our prayer time. Now, it is obvious that you need to be selective in the verses you choose, as something with a lot of "begets" (like 1 Chronicles) won't offer much encouragement to you. The book of Psalms is a wonderful one to use, for it contains many verses of praise and worship to Him. *(Teacher: Pick a few verse examples to help explain this.)*

Sing to Jesus

How many of you enjoy singing? God loves to hear our voices lifted to Him in song! What are some of the songs that you enjoy singing to Jesus?

- **(Psalm 147:1 CEV)** *"Shout praises to the LORD! Our God is kind, and it is right and good to sing praises to him."*
- **(Psalm 146:2 KJV)** *"While I live will I praise the LORD: I will sing praises unto my God while I have any being."*
- **(1 Chronicles 16:8-9 KJV)** *"Give thanks unto the LORD, call upon his name, make known his deeds among the people. Sing unto him, sing psalms unto him, talk ye of all his wondrous works."*
- **(Psalm 30:4 KJV)** *"Sing unto the LORD, O ye saints of his, and give thanks at the remembrance of his holiness."*

You have often been told that prayer is an essential (or necessary) part of your relationship with God. Just as you need to make sure you have enough of the right food, rest, and exercise for your physical body every day, you must take care of your spiritual body, too. We must take time to talk to Jesus and read His Word every day!

Jesus loves to hear us pray! Sometimes, it is easy to become distracted. We all lead very busy lives, and there are times that it is difficult to forget about the things that happened during our day. I believe that this new prayer tool will help us focus on what is important. I'm excited about using it, aren't you?

HOW DO I SHOW PRAISE TO GOD?

Lesson suggestion: As you teach this lesson, have the children join you in expressing the forms of worship as you teach. This particular lesson can be great fun!

The Bible says in **Psalms 100:4**, *"Enter into his gates with thanksgiving, and into his courts with praise: be thankful unto him, and bless his name."* **(KJV)** Today, we are going to look at some of the ways that we can praise God. We all can show our praise to Him more than we do. He has been so good to us!

First, let's look at some of the ways we show praise to people around us. If we go to a concert and we like the performance, what do we do? (Clap) If we are at a ballgame and someone scores a point, how do we react? (Cheer) If a child sees his/her parent and wants to be held, what happens? (He/she raises his/her hands, reaching out to the parent.) If someone wants to take you someplace exciting, do you ever jump up and down, cheer, or dance around the room because you are excited? Did you know that each of these actions is a type of praise? Did you know that Jesus likes it when you do that for Him, too? Let's look at the Bible and see what it says about praise. As we learn about what the Bible says, we are going to practice!

Clapping

(Psalm 47:1-2 WEB) *"Oh clap your hands, all you nations. Shout to God with the voice of triumph! For Yahweh Most High is awesome. He is a great King over all the earth."*

If your favorite singer was giving a concert, and you really liked the song he/she had just sang, would you clap? Yes! This is how we show how much we liked the song! Do you approve of God and all of the good things He has done for you? Let us clap our hands and show our approval to Jesus! (Clap) He does not *need* our approval, but He certainly enjoys getting it! What about you? Do you enjoy it when you are shown approval?

Shouting

(Psalm 47:1-2 WEB) *"Oh clap your hands, all you nations. Shout to God with the voice of triumph! For Yahweh Most High is awesome. He is a great King over all the earth."*

At Jericho: (Joshua 6:20 KJV) *"When the people heard the sound of the horns, they shouted as loud as they could. Suddenly, the walls of Jericho collapsed, and the Israelites charged straight into the city from every side and captured it."* Because they shouted praises to God, He gave them a great victory!

When the Israelites were fighting the Philistines: (1 Samuel 4:5-8 GW) *"When the LORD's ark came into the camp, all Israel shouted so loudly that the earth rang with echoes. As the Philistines heard the noise, they asked, "What's [all] this shouting in the Hebrew camp" The Philistines found out that the LORD's ark had come into the camp. Then they were frightened and said, "A god has come into [their] camp." They also said, "Oh no! Nothing like this has ever happened before. We're in trouble now! Who can save us from the power of these mighty gods? These are the gods who struck the Egyptians with every kind of plague in the desert."*

The Philistines heard of the way that God had punished the Egyptians, and this made them very afraid! Did you know that Satan and the other demons are afraid when you shout praises to God?

Now, why can't I just be calm and praise Him? (Imitate someone timidly praising God) If you were watching your friend play a game, and they were getting a lot of points, how would you praise them? Would you very quietly say (act timid), "You know, I think you have been doing a good job." No! You would be saying (loudly), "Great job! Way to go! You're the best!" Why? We show our excitement by raising our voice, by shouting loudly! Has Jesus done something for you that deserves loud praise? Let's shout our praises to Him right now! (Worship loudly)

Raising our hands

Have you ever noticed that a baby (or young child) always wants to be picked up by their parents? Why? Could it be because they trust their parents? Maybe they feel safe when their parents hold them! Do you feel safe when you know Jesus is taking care of you? I do! Let's look at a time when the Israelites fought against the Amalekites: *"So Joshua did as Moses had said to him, and fought with Amalek: and Moses, Aaron, and Hur went up to the top of the hill. And it came to pass, when Moses held up his hand, that Israel prevailed; and when he let down his hand, Amalek prevailed. But Moses' hands were heavy; and they took a stone, and put it under him, and he sat thereon; and Aaron and Hur stayed up his hands, the one on the one side, and the other on the other side; And his hands were steady until the going down of the sun. And Joshua discomfited Amalek and his people with the edge of the sword. And Jehovah said unto Moses, Write this for a memorial in a book, and rehearse it in the ears of Joshua: that I will utterly blot out the remembrance of Amalek from under heaven. And Moses built an altar, and called the name of it Jehovah-nissi..."* **(Exodus 17:10-15 ASV)**

Notice that in verse 15, it says Moses named the altar "Jehovah-nissi," which means "The Lord my Banner." In war, a soldier was given the job of carrying a banner that showed the victories won by that particular army. Also, when we raise our hands, we are telling God that we surrender to Him. I am sure that we could all win more victories if we surrendered more control of our lives to Jesus!

Leaping

Have you ever been so excited that all you could do is jump up and down? You just couldn't sit still! When Jesus was teaching what we call the Beatitudes, He ended them with this verse in **Luke 6:23**: *"Rejoice ye in that day, and leap for joy: for, behold, your reward is great in heaven: for in the like manner did their fathers unto the prophets."* **(KJV)**

When Peter told the lame man at the gate to the temple to rise and walk, guess what He did? *"And he leaping up stood, and walked, and entered with them into the temple, walking, and leaping, and praising God."* **(Acts 3:8 KJV)** Would you be excited if you had never walked, and then God healed you? What a miracle! He did not even need to learn to walk; God immediately gave the knowledge to him! What would you do? Slowly, stand up and walk slowly into the temple, and act like "It's no big deal? I am just walking for the first time in my life; what is all the fuss?" No! You would be jumping around, probably running to everyone and yelling, "Look at me! Look at me! I can walk!" Do you have anything to be excited about? Do you have a house to live in, clothes to wear, and food to eat? We all have at least one thing to be excited about: we awakened this morning with another day to live here on earth! We have much to be excited about! (Have everyone think of one thing for which they are thankful; then, have everyone practice leaping for joy!)

Read 2 Samuel 6:13-16 in order to illustrate the following. This trip was about 15 miles long. To help you relate to this distance, we will use a pace to equal one of my steps. If I took big steps, it would take about 26,400 steps to walk the 15 miles. This means that they stopped **4,400 times** to sacrifice to God. Now, for those of you that feel that you are "too cool" to jump and dance, please note: This was **King David** who was dancing — the ruler of all the Jews! If it was good for King David to dance, it is good for us to dance also!

We need to be expressive in our worship. If I stood here and taught you using one tone, meaning that my voice stayed the same all of the time, would you think I was excited? No! (You would probably think that I was a very boring teacher!) Let's show Jesus how happy we are that He lives in our heart, and let's keep practicing what we learned tonight!

CONSIDER THE SPIDER

Lesson suggestion: Whiteboard, markers.

How many of you don't understand why you are encouraged to pray often? How many feel that God doesn't answer your prayers, and that He doesn't really hear you?

Why do we need to read the Bible? You may say, "It is so difficult to read. There are so many funny words, and I just don't understand what I am reading." You might think, "Why do I need to pray? It seems like such work. It is so hard to concentrate. I could be playing my new computer game, or…" Sometimes, adults use excuses, too. We may not spend time playing video games, but we have plenty of other things to do that can draw our attention away from God, if we let them.

So, why are prayer and Bible reading so important?

What does the Bible say about reading God's Word?

It gives you power over sin. *"Thy word have I hid in mine heart, that I might not sin against thee."* **(Psalms 119:11 KJV)** *"Thy word is a lamp unto my feet, and a light unto my path."* **(Psalm 119:105 KJV)** *"Order my steps in thy word: and let not any iniquity have dominion over me."* **(Psalms 119:133 KJV)**

It gives life to your spirit. When Jesus was tempted to turn stones into bread, he quoted **Deuteronomy 8:3** *"…man doth not live by bread only, but by every word that proceedeth out of the mouth of the LORD doth man live."* **(KJV)** That is sort of hard to understand, isn't it? Listen to this version: *"… people do not live by bread alone; rather, we live by every word that comes from the mouth of the LORD."* **(NLT)** If you have a hard time understanding the words in your Bible, ask if you can try reading a different translation. (The GOD'S WORD version is written on an easy-to-understand, fourth-grade level.)

What does the Bible say about prayer?

It gives us strength to conquer our enemy. When the disciples could not cast a devil out of a child **(Matthew 17:14-20)**, Jesus answered by saying in **Matthew 17:21,** *"…this kind goeth not out but by prayer and fasting."* **(KJV)**

It develops our relationship with God. Have you ever heard the story about Cornelius? God sent an angel to Cornelius, who then told him to send for the Apostle Peter. You see, the Jewish apostles were not yet trying to reach the Gentiles (people who were not Jews). The prayers and the life of Cornelius, who did not have the Holy Ghost, made God want to pour His spirit out on him and his family; He simply needed a man to be His messenger. *"…Cornelius, thy prayer is heard, and thine alms are had in remembrance in the sight of God."* **(Acts 10:31 KJV)**

Now, can you possibly have a relationship with God without praying or reading the Bible? It would be extremely difficult! When prayer and reading God's Word are combined in a relationship with God, we become spiritually strong, and dealing with life's problems is much easier for us.

Let's consider a spider and how it lives. Have you ever watched one spin its web? The spider starts making what we call spokes. Once all of the spokes are in place, the spider then starts spinning circles that connect to the spokes. When the spokes and circles are complete, the spider simply sits in the middle of its web and waits for his prey! The web is sticky, which makes it very easy for the spider to trap its food. When an insect is caught in the web, the vibrations are felt in the center of the web; then, all the spider has to do is crawl over to the insect that is stuck, catch it, and eat!

Now, let us imagine that the spokes represent the times we spend putting God's Word in our hearts (Sunday School, church services, Bible reading, etc.). The circles are our prayers. Can you imagine the circles being able to support themselves without the spokes? It isn't possible! Just as the spider couldn't catch much dinner with only the spokes of a web, our relationship with God isn't complete without both prayer and Bible reading!

Prayer and Bible reading go together. You cannot separate one from the other and still have a healthy, balanced relationship with God.

Many times, we feel as if God has left us, when we truly are the ones that have left Him. We have not read His word or called upon His name. Living for God seems to get hard, and we lose our desire to pray or read His Word. We start to believe that it's okay to set those habits aside; after all, we have the Holy Ghost. We're "saved," so He'll understand if we don't worship, pray, or read and study His word, right? Wrong!

Keeping up the habit of prayer and Bible reading is sort of like our teeth-brushing habit. The dentist says that if you don't brush your teeth at least twice a day, you'll get cavities, and we all know that cavities are not a good thing! Just as a lack of brushing will lead to tooth decay, ignoring our relationship with God will lead to spiritual decay. **(Psalms 40:16 GW)** *"Let all who seek you rejoice and be glad because of you. Let those who love your salvation continually say, "The LORD is great!"* **(Psalms 119:9 GW)** *"How can a young person keep his life pure? He can do it by holding on to your word."*

HEARING GOD'S VOICE

Lesson suggestion: Whiteboard, markers.

As servants in God's kingdom, we need to be especially good at one thing: hearing His voice. You may ask, "How do you learn to hear God's voice? What does it sound like? How can we know when He speaks to us?"

1 Samuel mentions a boy who first heard God's voice when He was very young. Samuel was very special because he was a miracle baby. His mom had been unable to have children for a very long time. One day, she went to the temple and prayed for a long time. She promised the Lord that if He would give her a son, she would take him to serve in the temple when the boy was old enough. God saw the true desires of her heart, and answering her prayer by speaking to her through the priest, He promised Hannah that she would have a son.

The Bible does not tell how old Samuel was when his parents took him to the temple; we simply know that he was young. **Read 1 Samuel 3:1.**

One night, after he had gone to bed, Samuel heard a voice call his name. **Read 1 Samuel 3:1-10.**

The last part of verse 10 is very important. Samuel said, *"Speak; for your servant hears."* **(1 Samuel 3:10 WEB)** It is very important that we learn to listen for the voices of those who have authority over us (parents, teachers, pastor, etc.). Just as your mother and father teach you to listen and answer when they call for you, we must do the same with God. As His servants, we must always be ready to hear His voice. Because we are all different, He will speak to each of us in different ways. Your brother, sister, or friend may not hear Him the same way that you do, because we each have our own personal relationship with God! [Personal: of or relating to a particular person: PRIVATE <personal concerns>; concerning a particular individual's more intimate affairs, interests, or activities.][17]

In Old Testament times, God spoke to His people in many different ways. Here are just a few:

Through the leaders of Israel

- **(Exodus 35:4-21)** Moses told the people what God wanted them to give for the building of the temple.

By fire

- **(1 Kings 18:31-39)** Elijah's sacrifice was consumed before the prophets of Baal and all the children of Israel, showing everyone that God was the only one, true God!

By signs

- **(Exodus 15:22-26)** A bitter stream turned into sweet waters after a branch was thrown into it.
- **(Exodus 13:21)** God used pillars of fire and cloud to lead the Israelites out of Egypt.

By helping in battle

- **(Exodus 17:8-13)** Israelites won the battle as long as Moses' arms were raised; the sun stood still until Joshua defeated the Amorites. **(Joshua 10:12-13)**

---

[17] Webster's II New Riverside Dictionary, pg. 877.

How can we prepare ourselves to know His voice?

As you develop a relationship with someone, you begin to recognize their voice when you hear them speak, even if you aren't facing their direction. If they speak and you hear them, you know they are close by! When you were just a baby, you learned the sound of your mother's voice. You knew when she was near, and you knew when she walked away from you! Often, when a mother allows someone else to hold her baby, it begins to cry. Why? Because the person holding them is not familiar to them! The baby is probably thinking, "Who are you, why are you holding me, and where is my mother?" As we develop our relationship with God, we will begin to learn His voice.

How will we know when He speaks? How does He speak to us?

God will most likely not speak in a big, booming voice, and He probably won't ever set the top of a mountain on fire to get your attention! Rather, His words appear in your mind and they will have a distinct sound. As you get more comfortable in listening to God speak, you will become so familiar with His voice that you will not doubt whether or not you hear Him. We must learn to be quiet in God's presence and listen for His voice. It will be distinct (clear) and will sound the same each time that He speaks to you. God deals with each of us differently, so His voice will not sound the same to everyone.

If your mother is trying to talk to you, can you hear what she is saying if you are speaking at the same time? Most likely not! This is also true when we are talking with God. If we do all of the talking, how can He speak to us? He can't! We must learn how to be still and quiet, because it is during the quiet times in prayer that God is able to talk to us the best.

Why would He speak to us?

Listen to this: *"One night the Lord said to Paul in a vision, "Don't be afraid to speak out! Don't be silent! I'm with you. No one will attack you or harm you. I have many people in this city."* **(Acts 18:9-10 GW)** The Bible tells many instances of when God spoke to man. Why would He want to do this? To offer comfort when we are hurting, sad, or lonely; to give a word of knowledge (or information) so that we can better understand something; to give us direction when He wants us to do a job for Him (this could be praying for someone else who is hurting, or volunteering to help someone who is in need).

Why wouldn't you want God to speak to you?

If your mother or father lived in your house, yet never spoke to you, how would you feel? (Very sad!) Well, it's the same way with God. If you have a daily relationship with Him, then you will want Him to talk to you.

He wants to be able to speak to you!

God has been trying to talk to man ever since Adam and Eve were created. *"And they heard the voice of the LORD God walking in the garden in the cool of the day: and Adam and his wife hid themselves from the presence of the LORD God amongst the trees of the garden."* **(Genesis 3:8 KJV)** Since that time, absolutely nothing has changed! God wants nothing more than to talk to you every day. Unfortunately, we let ourselves get too busy with life. Many times, we don't give Him a chance to speak to us.

Think about it. God sits on His throne and waits for you to talk to Him! He can't heal you if you don't ask, He can't lead you if you don't want to be guided, and He can't speak to you if you don't listen. Won't you give Him a chance to talk to you? He's waiting!

WHAT IS INTERCESSION?

Lesson suggestion: Whiteboard, markers.

Warfare = "Fighting"; Travail = "Birthing"; Supplication = "Pleading"

We have learned how important prayer is to our relationship with God. Did you also know that if we allow God to show us how to pray, our prayers will become powerful? You may have heard stories about how someone felt led to pray for a missionary on the other side of the world, only to learn later that the missionary's life had been in danger while they had been praying! Have you ever wondered how you can pray powerful prayers like that?

Today, we are going to talk about how God can direct your prayers. We call this intercession, which means to make an intense (strong) appeal or request about something, or for someone. In **Romans 8:26** it says, *"Likewise the Spirit also helps in our weaknesses. For we do not know what we should pray for as we ought, but the Spirit Himself intercedes for us with inexpressible groanings."* **(EMTV)** Adults have names for the different types of intercession: Warfare, travail, and supplication. *We are going to call them "Fighting, Birthing, and Pleading."*

Fighting

Let's start with *fighting*. This type of fighting is good, because God is using our prayers to fight against Satan's forces. We call this "getting mad at the devil." When God uses us to fight, we will feel His emotions. This is why we may feel angry while praying, even if we don't know *why* we are angry. Our words may be forceful and we may not have tears. How do you act when you are arguing with someone? When fighting in your prayers, you may feel the same way.

(Ephesians 6:12 CEV) *"We are not fighting against humans. We are fighting against forces and authorities and against rulers of darkness and powers in the spiritual world."* However, there is no reason to be afraid. Paul also tells us in **1 Corinthians 10:3-4**, *"We are human, but we don't wage war with human plans and methods. We use God's mighty weapons, not mere worldly weapons, to knock down the Devil's strongholds."* **(NLT)**

Birthing

When God uses you in *birthing* intercession, you may feel sad. It may feel as though the words are being pulled out of your stomach, and they may be hard to say. You will most likely have tears running down your face.

Have you ever heard your mother talk about giving birth to you? It is possible that you have heard another adult describe the process of giving birth. When a woman gives birth to a baby, it is not always a pleasant process because there is a lot of pain involved. However, once the mother sees her new baby, she most likely forgets all about the pain that she had! *The baby is worth much more than the pain experienced while giving birth.* We experience this type of prayer when God wants to birth (or start) something new. He may be using you to birth a new desire for Him in one of your friends. God may want you to reach out to someone in your family who doesn't know Jesus, and He may choose to help you do this by having you pray a birthing type of prayer. He may also want to birth you into a new level of relationship with Him (teach you new things).

In travailing, or birthing, intercession, you may be begging for someone's protection, healing, or even his or her salvation. Jesus tells us to expect this type of prayer. **(John 16:20-22 BBE)** *"Truly I say to you, You will be weeping and sorrowing, but the world will be glad: you will be sad, but your sorrow will be turned into joy. When a woman is about to give birth she has sorrow, because her hour is come; but when she has given birth to the child, the pain is put out of her mind by the joy that a man has come into the world. So you have sorrow now: but I will see you again, and your hearts will be* *glad, and no one will take away your joy."* Did you notice that He also said, *"No one will take your joy away?"* We may feel sad while praying a birthing prayer, but it doesn't mean that we will feel sad *every* time that we pray. We simply experience God's emotions during this kind of prayer.

Another example is found in Paul's letter to the church in Galatia. He wrote in **Galatians 4:19-21**, *"My children, of whom I am again in birth-pains till Christ is formed in you, Truly my desire is to be present with you now, using a changed voice; for I am troubled about you. Say, you whose desire it is to be under the law, do you not give ear to the law?"* **(BBE)** Paul was telling them that God has prayed for them, through him, because of some problems they were having.

Pleading

I'm *sure* I don't have to go in an explanation about pleading! To plead means *"to urge reasons for or against; to attempt to persuade one by argument or supplication."*[18] Are there any pleading experts in this room? As soon as you walk into a store, do you begin begging your parents to buy whatever catches your eye? Many children do this, and it is especially noticeable in the checkout line. Every store manager seems to know exactly what little children will want to take home with them, because there are always interesting things located near the place where the parents have to pay for what they buy. It's likely that every parent has had to listen to their child plead for candy, or something else, while they wait in line.

You see, pleading intercession comes from your heart. When God uses you in this type of prayer, you are praying for needs with God's words. Paul wrote in **1 Timothy 2:1-2**, *"My desire is, first of all, that you will make requests and prayers and give praise for all men; For kings and all those in authority; so that we may have a calm and quiet life in all fear of God and serious behaviour."* **(BBE)** He also tells us in **Philippians 4:6**, *"Don't worry about anything, but in all your prayers ask God for what you need, always asking him with a thankful heart."* **(GNT)**

It is important for us to allow God to direct our prayers. When we allow Him to lead us, our prayers become powerful. Paul tells us in **Ephesians 6:18** to *"Pray in the Spirit in every situation. Use every kind of prayer and request there is. For the same reason be alert. Use every kind of effort and make every kind of request for all of God's people."* **(GW)**

When you pray in the Spirit, you never have to worry about using the right words, or praying about the right things. *When God gives you the words to say, they are always right.* In addition, by using God's words, you are using His faith. Remember, God used words to create the heavens and the earth.

Let's look at Paul's letter to the Christians at Ephesus. **(Ephesians 6:10-20 BBE)** *"Lastly, be strong in the Lord, and in the strength of his power. Take up God's instruments of war, so that you may be able to keep your position against all the deceits of the Evil One. For our fight is not against flesh and blood, but against authorities and powers, against the world-rulers of this dark night, against the spirits of evil in the heavens. For this reason take up all the arms of God, so that you may be able to be strong in the evil day, and, having done all, to keep your place. Take your place, then, having your body clothed with the true word, and having put on the breastplate of righteousness; Be ready with the good news of peace as shoes on your feet; And most of all, using faith as a cover to keep off all the flaming arrows of the Evil One. And take salvation for your head-dress and the sword of the Spirit, which is the word of God: With prayers and deep desires, making requests at all times in the Spirit, and keeping watch, with strong purpose, in prayer for all the saints, And for me, that words may be given to me in the opening of my mouth, to make clear without fear the secret of the good news, For which I am a representative in chains, and that I may say without fear the things which it is right for me to say."*

---

[18] Noah Webster's 1828 Dictionary of American English

It is important to notice that prayer is actually a part of the armor of God. Just as we need to be sure that we ask God to apply the other parts of His armor to our lives, we need to make prayer a part of our daily lives, too. **(Ephesians 6:11-18)** Intercession is one of the ways that we can make our prayers powerful.

- **(Matthew 6:6 KJV)** *"But thou, when thou prayest, enter into thy closet, and when thou hast shut thy door, pray to thy Father which is in secret; and thy Father which seeth in secret shall reward thee openly."*
- **(James 5:16b KJV)** *"The effectual fervent prayer of a righteous man availeth much."*
- **(Psalms 55:17 KJV)** *"Evening, and morning, and at noon, will I pray, and cry aloud: and he shall hear my voice."*

OUR SPIRITUAL ICE CREAM SUNDAE:
Exploring the Fruits of the Spirit

Lesson suggestion: Whiteboard, colored markers; you will be drawing an ice cream sundae. Another illustration option: using construction paper or poster board cut out the different "parts" of a sundae. Tape it to the wall (or whatever is available), adding each piece as you teach. If you feel adventurous, you could offer ice cream at the close of your lesson!

Let's think of our relationship with God as an ice cream sundae. I'm going to draw as I talk, and I would like for you to help me!

The bowl represents our life. The three scoops of ice cream represent the steps of Salvation. Chocolate = Repentance, Strawberry = Baptism, and Vanilla = the Holy Ghost.

(Draw a sundae on the whiteboard as you teach.) Okay, there is our ice cream sundae! Now, we need to put toppings on it. These will represent the things that are added to our lives as we begin to grow in our relationship with God. *Encourage involvement from the children: what toppings do they like on their ice cream sundae? How would their toppings relate to a spiritual attribute? Only a few attributes are listed due to a lack of space. Encourage feedback! What do your students think will be added as they grow in God?*

Syrup = Joy; Cherries = Wisdom; Sprinkles = Spiritual gifts; Nuts = Boldness in witnessing to friends & others

As we grow in God, He begins to add good things to our life that help us in our Christian walk. There are many great things that God would like to share with us. **Galatians 5:22, 23** says, *"But the fruit of the Spirit is love, joy, peace, longsuffering, gentleness, goodness, faith, meekness, temperance: against such there is no law."* **(KJV)** Let's list these on the board *(discuss each one as you write)*.

- ***Love:*** *"In a general sense to be pleased with; to regard with affection..."*[19] **(Matthew 22:36-39)**
- ***Joy:*** *"The passion or emotion excited by the acquisition or expectation of good; To rejoice; to be glad; to exult."*[20] **(Psalm 16:11)**
- ***Peace:*** *"In a general sense, a state of quiet or tranquility; freedom from disturbance or agitation;"*[21] **(Romans 8:6)**
- ***Longsuffering:*** *"Bearing injuries or provocation for a long time; patient; not easily provoked."*[22] **(Psalm 86:15)**
- ***Gentleness:*** *"Softness of manners; mildness of temper; sweetness of disposition; meekness."*[23] **(2 Samuel 22:36)**
- ***Goodness:*** *"The state of being good; the physical qualities which constitute value, excellence or perfection;"*[24] **(Psalm 23:6)**
- ***Faith:*** *"Belief; the assent of the mind to the truth of what is declared by another, resting on his authority and veracity, without other evidence; the judgment that what another states or testifies is the truth."*[25] **(Mark 11:22)**
- ***Meekness:*** *"Softness of temper; mildness; gentleness; forbearance under injuries and provocations."*[26] **(Titus 3:2)**

---

[19] Noah Webster's 1828 Dictionary of American English
[20] Noah Webster's 1828 Dictionary of American English
[21] Noah Webster's 1828 Dictionary of American English
[22] Noah Webster's 1828 Dictionary of American English
[23] Noah Webster's 1828 Dictionary of American English
[24] Noah Webster's 1828 Dictionary of American English
[25] Noah Webster's 1828 Dictionary of American English
[26] Noah Webster's 1828 Dictionary of American English

- ***Temperance***: *"Patience; calmness;"*[27] *(self-control)* **(2 Peter 1:5-7)**

God wants us to have all of these wonderful things in our lives, and as we submit ourselves to Him, these fruits will begin to show up!

What else do you think God has to offer us? **Read 1 Corinthians 12:8-10.** *"For to one is given by the Spirit the word of wisdom; to another the word of knowledge by the same Spirit; To another faith by the same Spirit; to another the gifts of healing by the same Spirit; To another the working of miracles; to another prophecy; to another discerning of spirits; to another divers kinds of tongues; to another the interpretation of tongues:"* Once we have grown in our relationship with God to the point that He believes He can trust us with something very special, He bestows gifts upon us! Let's write these on the board, too.

- **Word of knowledge:** *special information that comes only from God about someone or something*
- **Word of wisdom:** *ability given by God that tells you how to use knowledge*
- **Discerning of spirits:** *ability given by God to know what spirits are at work*
- **Gift of faith:** *ability to believe God and to transfer, or give, that faith to others*
- **Gift of healing:** *ability to lay hands on someone and they be healed*
- **Gift of miracles:** *ability to pray, believe, and see miracles happen*
- **Diverse kinds of tongues**: *ability to pray in tongues at any time (this could be for personal benefit or for many to receive, as in a church service)*
- **Interpretation of tongues:** *ability to interpret an utterance of diverse kinds of tongues for the benefit of many (as in a church service)*
- **Gift of prophecy:** *ability to convey (or deliver) God's word or reveal God's word for the future*

These explanations will do for now. Later, we will have another lesson that explains each of these more thoroughly.

Now, how many of you like to receive gifts? Oh, yes! I do, too! My birthday is my favorite day for presents! What is the *best* gift that you have *ever* received? (*Student feedback*) Now, what was God's best gift to you? That's right, it was the Holy Ghost! The Bible says that we should desire the spiritual gifts that we talked about earlier. **(1 Corinthians 14:1)** However, I have a question. Do you think He would be interested in giving us His gifts if we aren't doing our best for Him all of the time? Probably not, right?

Let's take another look at our ice cream sundae. I have some more topping suggestions! What about *chili powder*? I know, we need *pepper and salt*! Surely, that would taste wonderful! Oh, and we can't forget the *garlic... Why, what's wrong*? Some of you don't sound very interested in my toppings! Doesn't it sound tasty to you? No? Let's talk about this for a minute. I'm going to make another list.

Chili Powder = Gossip; Garlic = Lying; Pepper = Cheating; Salt = Disobedience
(Suggest other toppings and negative attributes)

What would these toppings do to your ice cream sundae? That's right, they would ruin it completely! If you ate it, you would most likely get a stomachache! I wonder how God feels about us when we add something to our life that makes Him sad. Do you think that our actions sometimes give Him a heartache?

---

[27] Noah Webster's 1828 Dictionary of American English

We are all human and we make mistakes. God knows this. However, I have a question. When we have the chance to create a tasty ice cream sundae out of our life, why would we want to ruin it with all of the bad stuff that Satan has to offer us? It just doesn't make much sense, does it? We should work to present our lives as a tasty treat to the Lord, making sure that it's one that is pleasant and filled with the fruits of the Spirit. He will help us; we just need to ask Him!

LIVING A FRUIT-FULL LIFE

Lesson suggestion: Create four separate pictures of a tree using a flannel graph or poster board, etc. Stage 1: Portray a healthy tree with many leaves. Stage 2: The tree begins to have just a few worms infest its leaves. Stage 3: The tree is completely infested with worms. Stage 4: The tree is now dying and its leaves are completely brown and withered. Write "habit words" (such as "lying," "music," "disobedience," etc.) on the worm-infested leaves. This can be used as a powerful illustration to show the children how certain habits or behaviors can adversely affect their lives.

There are three things that we must do in order to live a fruitful life for God.

1. We must repent of our sins, which means that we choose to change our habits and no longer do the bad (or wrong) things that we used to do.

2. We must be baptized in Jesus name. When we are baptized, we go all the way down in the water and get completely wet; the preacher baptizing us says, "I baptize you in the name of Jesus Christ." This means we now carry Jesus' name on our hearts! When we are baptized, our sins are washed away, and all of the bad things that we've done are gone, too!

3. After we're baptized, we must pray and ask Jesus for the Holy Ghost! When our heart has been cleaned from all of the sins that we have committed, God can put His spirit inside of us. When He moves into our heart to stay, the proof is found in the sign that God gives to us: we will speak in another language that we have never learned. Once this happens, it means that Jesus will be with us all of the time!

Once we've followed these three steps, it's very important that we try to do our best all of the time.

When we receive the Holy Ghost and begin to work on our relationship with God, the fruits of the Spirit will start to work in our life. **Galatians 5:22-23** says: *"But the fruit of the Spirit is **love, joy, peace, longsuffering, gentleness, goodness, faith, meekness, temperance**: against such there is no law."* **(KJV)**

Now, let's pretend that our Christian life is like a tree. When we do the best we can, and we work at being a good Christian, our tree is healthy! In order to keep it that way, we must pray, read our Bible, and study God's Word. When we do these things, our tree will begin to bear spiritual fruit.

Sometimes life can get hard, and we may start to slip a little in different things. We forget to pray! Oh, we used to do it every day, because we started a good habit when we were filling out our 21-day-habit prayer chart.* Maybe we think that God won't care if we miss talking to Him for a few days. We may forget to read our Bible, too, but we're sure that God doesn't mind if we miss just a few days...

"Oh, did you hear that great rock song the other day? I know my mom wouldn't like it, because it sort of has a few bad words, but I think the music is really cool, so I just plug my ears when those words come on." We've just allowed a worm to bite into the fruit on our tree! If we don't remove the worm, or change the bad habit that we've just started, things will just get worse! "Oops, I didn't mean to say that bad word. I guess I just got used to hearing it in that song and it sort of slipped out just then. Sorry!"

Song of Solomon 2:15 says, *"Catch for us the foxes, the little foxes that ruin the vineyards, our vineyards that are in bloom."* **(KJV)** I looked this up in a Bible dictionary, and it compared the foxes to a caterpillar that ruins a vine!

"Hey, did you see that movie the other day? I sure don't want my mom to know I watched it. There were some things in it that I know she wouldn't have approved of, but you know, I think I'm old enough to make some decisions like that. As long as I close my eyes during those bad parts, I'm sure it'll be okay." Uh, oh! There's another worm.

Eventually, we may let so many bad habits poison our spiritual fruit that our tree (relationship with Jesus) begins to die. If it gets to that point, there are two things we can do:

1. We can choose to simply not be concerned about the consequences of our actions. Soon, our spiritual tree will be completely diseased. If we are not careful to always keep good habits, it can be easy for this to happen.

2. We can decide to "prune" our tree and remove the branches that are spiritually dead. We do this by repenting and asking Jesus to wash our hearts clean. Remember, we must do more than simply ask Jesus for forgiveness; we must also choose to change our habits! Once we repent, we should also seek to speak in our Holy Ghost language again. God's Spirit will act as the "purifying spray" that makes us righteous before Him once more.

What does our life look like? Is it fruitful? Do we have the fruits of the Spirit? Do we show love and kindness toward others? Do we do our best to read our Bible and pray every day, or is our life like a poisoned tree that is almost beyond hope? If we could see God looking at us right now, would He be happy, or sad?

Note to Teacher: This would be a good time to encourage the children in their goal of completing the 21-day habit prayer chart distributed at the end of the previous lesson.

PUTTING ON THE ARMOR OF GOD

Lesson suggestion: Make your own "armor" using poster board, cutting out each piece and decorating as needed; silver or yellow are great colors because they resemble precious metals. You can make it as fun as you want, possibly even using glitter wording to label and beautify your "armor" ("Salvation, Shield of Faith," etc.). To enable wearing of the "armor," you can attach long pieces of ribbon to the sides of each piece as needed by using brads; this will enable you to fit the armor to all shapes and sizes of kids!

Alternate idea: an area Christian Book Store may have a child's set of armor available for sale.

Today, we are going to talk about putting on the armor of God. I have a question to ask you before we start: do we really know what it means to be a Christian?

Have you ever heard anyone talk about putting on the armor of God? What does it mean to have our loins girt about with truth? What is the helmet of salvation?

Ephesians 6:11-18 (MKJV)

Verse 11: *"Put on the whole armor of God so that you may be able to stand against the wiles of the devil.*

- "Wiles" means trickery or deceit by someone that is untruthful in order to "get their way."

Verse 12: *"For we do not wrestle against flesh and blood, but against principalities, against powers, against the world's rulers, of the darkness of this age, against spiritual wickedness in high places."*

- "Principalities" is a big word that refers to the rulers of what we would call the "dark world," the spirits that do the devil's "dirty work."

Verse 13: *"Therefore take to yourselves the whole armor of God, that you may be able to withstand in the evil day, and having done all, to stand."*

- When we pray and ask God to put His armor upon us, we are literally asking for God's personal protection. The wonderful thing about this is that He is always ready to protect us from evil! He really loves us!

Verse 14: *"Therefore stand, having your loins girded about with truth,..."*

- What is truth? It is God's Word! This is why you should read your Bible and memorize verses, for it gives your spiritual armor *power*!

Verse 14: *"...and having on the breastplate of righteousness;"*

- Righteousness is a big word that simply means "right living." We need to live in a way that is pleasing to God. A good way to remember this is to ask yourself the question, "What would Jesus think about this?" "How would Jesus act in this situation?" If we are concentrating on making sure that our choices match the Word of God, then God will be pleased with what we say, do, or think.

Verse 15: *"and your feet shod with the preparation of the gospel of peace."*

- These spiritual shoes help you to always be ready to share "peace" with others. Everyone wants to have peace (not feeling troubled, or being upset). When we allow Jesus to be the most important part of our lives, we become a messenger of His peace!

Verse 16: *"Above all, take the shield of faith, with which you shall be able to quench all the fiery darts of the wicked."*

- Our faith in God keeps us protected from all of the bad things that the devil tries to do to us. *(Teacher: giving a personal testimony of a healing, a miraculous change in a drastic situation, or some other faith-building example will help illustrate this point.)*

Verse 17: *"And take the helmet of salvation…"*

- Our salvation acts like an invisible helmet on our head. When the Holy Ghost is actively working in our lives, we can pray and ask God to protect the thoughts that our mind produces. God's Spirit gives us the right to tell our spiritual enemy to leave us alone. We can tell him to stop putting bad thoughts in our mind, and he has to listen to us!

Verse 17: *"and the sword of the Spirit, which is the Word of God:"*

- The Sword of the Spirit is our weapon! The devil hates the Word of God, and he's even scared of it! When we quote God's Word to him, he has to listen and obey what it says. Now, think about something that scares you (e.g. bumblebees, spiders, etc.). Imagine how that "scary thing" makes you feel. Guess what: The devil is more afraid of God's Word than you could ever be! *Teacher, you can personalize this by sharing a personal experience.*

Verse 18: *"Praying always with all prayer and supplication in the Spirit…"*

- When speaking about the armor of God, we definitely can't forget this verse! When a soldier goes into battle, he needs strength and endurance. If he is physically tired or weak, he will not be able to use his weapon effectively, and all of the armor in the world won't save him if he doesn't have the strength to fight his enemy. As for us, if we do not pray, we will not have the power (or strength) within us to stand against the temptations of the devil. Prayer is a very effective weapon!

- Our prayer time is very important. Each time we pray with our friends, it strengthens our friendships and helps our love for others grow. When we are having a problem, praying with friends will also help us feel stronger. **(Matthew 18:19-20 CEV)** *"I promise that when any two of you on earth agree about something you are praying for, my Father in heaven will do it for you. Whenever two or three of you come together in my name, I am there with you."*

- We must also remember that it is very important to pray every day, not just when we go to church services. Here's an example: A situation at school happens on Tuesday. Do you want to wait until the next church service to talk to Jesus about it? That could be days later! Why not take a minute to walk into the restroom at school and pray silently? God hears you all of the time, and it only takes a minute to ask for His help. Sometimes, just saying His name takes care of our problem!

- Even adults need to choose to pray! Teaching Sunday School or singing in the choir doesn't automatically create a prayer life for us. God doesn't give us the Holy Ghost, and then hand us an invisible schedule while saying, "Okay, (name). Now that you have the Holy Ghost, you will pray at 9:00 a.m. on Sundays, 2:45 p.m. on Mondays, and let's see… on Wednesdays, you will pray at 3:15 p.m." That sounds silly, but I'm sure that you understand what I mean! God will not ever make us pray or read His Word, because He gave each of us the ability to choose what we want to do. We have to create these habits ourselves, and we do it by setting aside time for Jesus each day. It helps if we develop a habit and pray at the same time every day, but our lives don't always work that way. God understands! It doesn't matter to Him when you do it, He just wants you to **do** it.

God loves you, and He will honor your effort!

TEMPTATION:
Can We Stand Against It?

Lesson suggestion: Whiteboard, markers.

As Christians, we face temptation every day. It may be an extra cookie that we didn't have permission to eat, watching TV when we should be doing homework or chores, or listening to a CD (or something on the internet) that we know would displease both God and our parents. Let's learn what the Bible says about temptation. You may be surprised at what we discover!

What is temptation?

(Synonyms: a trap, a test, or a lure) To "tempt" is to talk someone into doing something that isn't right, possibly by promising a reward if they do it.

Have you been tempted?

We are all tempted by things that we would like to have, or do, but shouldn't. We already mentioned some of them earlier. What about reading a book that we know is not suitable for a Christian? Or, taking a small piece of candy in the store when we know it's wrong? It is not possible for adults to watch you every second of every day, and there *will* be times that you are tempted! The Bible says that every man is tempted when he is drawn away by his own desires. **Read James 1:14**. [To lust means to have a great want for something, such as money.]

Was Jesus Tempted?

(Read Matthew 4:1-11 and Hebrews 4:15) Following His baptism by John the Baptist, Jesus stayed in the wilderness and fasted for 40 days. Satan came to Jesus during this time and tempted Him with many things: food, power, possessions, and Satan's worldly kingdom. All Satan required is that Jesus bow down and worship him! What a great and horrible price to pay! Jesus simply said to him, "Get out of here, Satan!" Jesus told him, *"For the Scriptures say, 'you must worship the Lord your God; serve only him."* **(Matthew 4:10 NLT)** Jesus was tempted, too!

How are we tempted?

Temptation is what happens when we desire to have something that is not good for us. However, *God does not tempt us.* **(James 1:13-15 NIV)** *"When tempted, no one should say, "God is tempting me." For God cannot be tempted by evil, nor does he tempt anyone; but each one is tempted when, by his own evil desire, he is dragged away and enticed. Then, after desire has conceived, it gives birth to sin; and sin, when it is full-grown, gives birth to death."* We are tempted simply because we are human, and we were all born into sin! **Read Psalm 51:5**.

Can we withstand temptation?

"There isn't any temptation that you have experienced which is unusual for humans. God, who faithfully keeps his promises, will not allow you to be tempted beyond your power to resist. But when you are tempted, he will also give you the ability to endure the temptation as your way of escape." **(1 Corinthians 10:13 GW)**

What should our attitude be toward temptation?

"My brothers and sisters, be very happy when you are tested in different ways. You know that such testing of your faith produces endurance. Endure until your testing is over. Then you will be mature and complete, and you won't need anything. Blessed are those who endure when they are tested. When they pass the test, they will receive the crown of life that God has promised to those who love him." **(James 1: 2-4, 12 GW)**

When we give into temptation, we often have to suffer the punishment for our actions, and that is never fun! As long as we are trying to live according to God's Word, we will fight against temptation. This is because our flesh does not like to submit to God! In **2 Corinthians 12:6-9,** Paul discusses his "thorn in the flesh." He asked God to remove it three times, and God's response was, *"My grace is sufficient for you."* Paul then said, *"My strength is made perfect in weakness."* This means that Paul was glad to suffer! We look at the Apostle Paul as being a great man, yet it appears that he had to endure this "thorn" for a very long time. Think about this for a moment. Do you think that Paul's willingness to suffer could have been the reason that his ministry was so blessed? We should also be glad that God sees us worthy to withstand temptation.

When we are filled with the Holy Ghost, our ability to stand up against temptation becomes much greater! **(Acts 1:8a; Ephesians 6:10)** But, when we try to do right by using our own power, we will nearly always fail. Only through God is our strength made perfect! *"The LORD is my light and my salvation; whom shall I fear? the LORD is the strength of my life; of whom shall I be afraid?"* **(Psalms 27:1 KJV)**

WHAT DOES IT MEAN TO BE HOLY?

Lesson suggestion: *You'll need a jar with lid, some cooking oil, several cups of water, clear drinking glass, chocolate milk powder or syrup, and 8 oz. milk.*

Note: *Because of the age of the children being taught, this lesson does not offer specifics regarding acceptable outward dress or appearance. Rather, it focuses on the inward matters of the heart, leaving the other instruction to be provided within the home. Consider speaking to your pastor about the guidelines he prefers to set for this lesson.*

We have all heard our pastor talk about being holy, or use the word "holiness," but what does that really mean?

Holiness is what we seek when we work hard to know God better. Many scriptures in the Bible talk about holiness. We *cannot* become holy all by ourselves. We have to want God's spirit, His presence, and His power in our lives! To be holy means to be separated from sin. Have you ever seen your mom separate an egg when she's baking something? It's just like that! **Leviticus 19:2** says *"Ye shall be holy: for I the Lord your God am holy."* **(KJV)** God wants us to be holy, but He surely won't make us that way. We have to **want** it!

When the Bible talks about God being holy, it refers to Him being perfect and good. There are different parts of ourselves that we must surrender to Him in order to have holiness in our life.

Our Heart

People will know if there is holiness in our heart. We won't have to tell them anything about ourselves at all! They will know whether or not we're holy by (1) how we act, (2) what we say, (3) what we do, and (4) by our attitude. All of these things put out a big advertisement that tells all about our "Heart Condition," kind of like those big flashing billboards you see next to the highway! King David said, *"Create in me a clean heart, O God; and renew a right spirit within me. Cast me not away from thy presence; and take not thy holy spirit from me."* **(Psalm 51:10-11 KJV)** The king did not want any of his bad attitudes or bad actions to keep him away from God's presence!

Ourselves

We need to be careful about how comfortable we become with things in the world. Some things that may seem pretty small to us are:

- TV shows with just a "few" bad words
- a movie with a part that we always have to "fast-forward" through
- a song with a really cool beat that may have bad words, or talk about things we shouldn't hear

None of these things will help make us spiritually healthy; rather, they'll make us "spiritually *sick*!" We cannot have things like this in our life and expect God to hug us with His presence! **2 Corinthians 6:17** says, *"Therefore come out from them and be separate, says the Lord. Touch no unclean thing, and I will receive you."* **(NIV)** ***(Teacher: mix the water and cooking oil in the jar to show how our spiritual life cannot mix with things of the world.)***

In Love

We should love one another! When we receive the Holy Ghost, we are filled with God's love. It is very important that we don't let this love "leak out!" Only when we pray and study God's Word can we fill up our heart's "love tank" (kind of like when you eat your favorite ice cream until you're completely stuffed)! **(1 John 4:7 KJV)** *"Beloved, let's love one another..."*

Our Speech

Many times people talk unkindly about someone, and then end up feeling badly afterwards. Have you ever felt like that? We should not gossip. Instead, we should help the "gossiper" break their bad habit! We should not complain; rather, we should be thankful!

(Ephesians 4:31, 32 NIV) *"Get rid of all bitterness, rage and anger, brawling and slander, along with every form of malice. Be kind and compassionate to one another, forgiving each other, just as in Christ God forgave you."*

Our Appearance

It is important that we do not look as the world does. If we do, how will our friends know that we are different? It would be hard to be a good witness to a friend who didn't know Jesus if we looked just like them. How could we explain the difference that He makes in our life? **(1 Samuel 16:7 KJV)** *"...for man looketh on the outward appearance, but the Lord looketh on the heart."*

The only way to become holy is to spend time with Him. Praying and reading God's Word are two important habits that we must have. They go together, just like chocolate syrup and milk! If you mix them together, you have chocolate milk! *"Taste and see that the LORD is good. Blessed is the person who takes refuge in him."* **(Psalms 34:8 GW)** *(Teacher: mix the chocolate milk and take a nice, big, long drink!)*

We cannot please God without holiness, and we cannot go to Heaven to see Him without it! **Matthew 5:8** says, *"Blessed are the pure in heart, for they shall see God."* **(KJV)** I want to see Him, don't you?

OUR ACTIONS: RIGHT OR WRONG?

Lesson suggestion: Whiteboard, markers.

Have you ever tasted homemade cookies, or enjoyed eating a pie made by someone in your home? Does your mom or grandma make special desserts for you to enjoy? Well, just like ingredients can make a recipe turn out great, or completely ruin it, there are times that our actions can "make or break" us!

We're going to create our own recipe for a good, healthy, Christian walk. Let's see how we do!

OUR CHRISTIAN WALK WITH GOD

<u>Ingredients</u>

- Make fun of others
- Share with our sibling(s)
- Kind
- Angry with a friend
- Thoughtful of others
- Rebellious to teachers
- Gossip about others
- Jealous of others
- Obedient to our parents
- Arguing with our sibling(s)

Whoa… Wait just a minute! Something tells me that this is a very bad recipe! What is wrong with it?

Is it really possible to be rebellious and kind at the same time? And, we couldn't possibly be thoughtful of others, yet be jealous of them, too! I think we need to see what the Bible has to say about some of these actions!

Act with kindness and patience (be kind to others; don't lose your temper)

(Proverbs 14:17 CEV) *"Fools have quick tempers, and no one likes you if you can't be trusted."* Hatred is a result of not being happy with ourselves. Many times, we end up taking our bad feelings out on other people. This is wrong! Also, if we are quick to become angry, we'll end up doing something we'll regret, and we probably won't have very many friends, either!

(Proverbs 15:18 CEV) *"Losing your temper causes a lot of trouble, but staying calm settles arguments."*

(Proverbs 14:30 CEV) *"It's healthy to be content, but envy can eat you up."* Envy is the same as jealousy, and God is not pleased with this!

(Ephesians 4:32 KJV) *"And be ye kind one to another, tenderhearted, forgiving one another, even as God for Christ's sake hath forgiven you."*

(Ephesians 5:2 CEV) *"Let love be your guide. Christ loved us and offered his life for us as a sacrifice that pleases God."*

Have respect for authority (honor those in positions of authority over you)

(Proverbs 13:1 NKJV) *"A wise son heeds his father's instruction, but a scoffer does not listen to rebuke."* (To heed means to listen; to scoff means to make fun of something.)

(Proverbs 12:1 NKJV) *"Whoever loves instruction loves knowledge, but he who hates correction is stupid."*

(Proverbs 8:33 KJV) *"Hear instruction, and be wise, and refuse it not."*

Be diligent (pay attention to one's work, responsibilities)

(Proverbs 6:6-8 NLT) *"Take a lesson from the ants, you lazybones. Learn from their ways and be wise! Even though they have no prince, governor, or ruler to make them work, they labor hard all summer, gathering food for the winter."*

We should be willing to take care of our responsibilities while still having a good attitude (e.g. cleaning our room without being told, taking out the trash, doing our homework, etc.).

Be "speech-conscious" (be aware of the words that we say)

(Proverbs 10:18 CEV) *"He that hideth hatred with lying lips, and he that uttereth slander, is a fool."* **(KJV)** *"You can hide your hatred by telling lies, but you are a fool to spread lies."*

(Proverbs 24:28-29 CEV) *"Don't accuse anyone who isn't guilty. Don't ever tell a lie or say to someone, "I'll get even with you!"*

(Proverbs 18:7-8) *"A fool's mouth is his destruction, and his lips are the snare of his soul. The words of a talebearer are as wounds, and they go down into the innermost parts of the belly."* **(KJV)** *"Saying foolish things is like setting a trap to destroy yourself. There's nothing so delicious as the taste of gossip! It melts in your mouth."* **(CEV)** Careless words (ones spoken being thoughtful) can hurt someone very deeply, so we must always be careful of what we say.

(Proverbs 11:13 CEV) *"A gossip tells everything, but a true friend will keep a secret."*

(James 3:8, 10 KJV) *"But the tongue can no man tame; it is an unruly evil, full of deadly poison. Out of the same mouth proceedeth blessing and cursing. My brethren, these things ought not so to be."*

(James 3:8-10 CEV) *"But our tongues get out of control. They are restless and evil, and always spreading deadly poison. My dear friends, with our tongues we speak both praises and curses. We praise our Lord and Father, and we curse people who were created to be like God, and this isn't right."*

(Proverbs 20:19 KJV) *"He that goeth about as a talebearer revealeth secrets: therefore meddle not with him that flattereth with his lips."* In other words, stay away from people who gossip!

(Colossians 4:6 KJV) *"Let your speech be always with grace, seasoned with salt, that ye may know how ye ought to answer every man."* Choose your words carefully!

(Philippians 4:8 KJV) *"Finally, brethren, whatsoever things are true, whatsoever things are honest, whatsoever things are just, whatsoever things are pure, whatsoever things are of good report; if there be any virtue, and if there be any praise, think on THESE things."*

Satan would love for us to "mess up" with our actions all of the time because it hurts our Christian witness! Why would someone who doesn't know Jesus want to be like us if we act in wrong ways all of the time? We need to make right choices, and Jesus promises to help us do this!

ATTITUDE:
Right or Wrong, We All Have One!

Lesson suggestion: Whiteboard, marker

As we grow in our walk with God, we will have situations happen that cause different types of reactions. *These reactions are either negative or positive, depending on our general attitude towards life!*

Example: Two friends play a game together. There are several different attitudes that each one can portray (or show) at the end of the game.

Winner

- Humble/Good sportsmanship: "You played a good game! Maybe you will win next time."
- Proud: "Well, I really deserved to win since I played better than you, anyway."

Loser

- Friendly/Good sportsmanship: "You know, you did play better than I did. You deserved to win."
- Sore Loser: "I can't believe I didn't win. I'm not playing this dumb game anymore!"

Which attitudes were right, and which were wrong?

There are two types of attitudes!

- ***Positive:*** Marked by certainty, acceptance, or affirmation; CONFIDENT <a positive attitude>[28]
- ***Negative:*** Lacking the quality of being positive; containing a negation or denial <a negative thought; a negative response>[29]

We need to be careful of our attitudes at all times! Simply attending every weekly church service will not make us a good disciple of Jesus! (What? Do you not think that you're a disciple of Christ?) If you have received the Holy Ghost, then yes, you are one of His disciples! God's Spirit is resident within (lives inside) you, and it is your job to help spread His love and His teachings. The definition of a disciple is *"one who believes in and helps disseminate [spread] the teachings of a master."*[30] What teachings are you spreading? Your actions speak much louder than any words you could say, and many times a bad attitude doesn't require words; a sad/mad/grumpy facial expression is enough! What do your actions and attitudes say to those who don't know Jesus?

Read 1 Corinthians 13:1-8. We need to be sure that we have the love of Jesus in our hearts, and that we show it to other people. We can accomplish many things in our life, but if His love isn't a part of us, the Bible says, "We are nothing!"

Read Galatians 5:22-23. Our lives should show the fruits of the Spirit *(love, joy, peace, longsuffering, gentleness, goodness, faith, meekness, and temperance).*

Question: *If the fruits of the Spirit are operating in our life, and we have a right attitude, will we do the following things?* (Yes or No)

- Gossip
- Talk against authority over us (rebel, or refuse to obey)
- Treat our family members and others badly

---

[28] Webster's II New Riverside Dictionary, pg. 918.
[29] Webster's II New Riverside Dictionary, pg. 788.
[30] Webster's II New Riverside Dictionary, pg. 383.

Question: *Is it possible to fake a good attitude?*

- Yes, it is!

Question: *How can you tell if someone is faking a good attitude?*

- You will eventually be able to tell if someone is faking a good attitude because they will not *always* be on their guard, and they will forget to "be a fake!" Someone who fakes a good attitude will change the way they act all of the time. You never know what they're going to say, or do, next!

(Proverbs 12:22 KJV) *"Lying lips are abomination to the Lord: but they that deal truly are His delight."*

(Proverbs 12:20 KJV) *"Deceit is in the heart of them that imagine evil…"*

Philippians 4:8 says, *"Finally, brethren, whatsoever things are true, whatsoever things are honest, whatsoever things are just, whatsoever things are pure, whatsoever things are of good report; if there be any virtue, and if there be any praise, think on THESE things."* **(KJV)**

There are several questions that can always help us in tough situations.

- *"How would Jesus respond to this situation?"*
- *"What would Jesus do?"*
- *"What would Jesus say?"*
- *"How would Jesus act?"*

If we are sincere in wanting to be more like Jesus, we simply have to ask Him; He is ready to help us with our attitude every day!

WHAT IS MY "HOLINESS GRADE?"

Lesson suggestion: We are looking at the difference between a true Christian and one that occasionally acts like one. *Visual aid needs:* Two fresh fruits or vegetables. One should be "old" (shrunken, wilted, or near rotten stage), and one should be ripe and looking good enough to eat! If an "old" one is not available, try this: using an apple, make a very small hole or incision at the bottom of the fruit; then, inject some dark food coloring into it. During the lesson, you can cut the apple apart to show how we can look the part of a Christian, but have a dirty heart on the inside.

A generous amount of scripture is included in this lesson, giving it a rather lengthy appearance. As repetition may occur on numerous occasions, the additional scriptures simply allow for variety. Therefore, don't feel as though you must include every single scripture when teaching it each time. This will also help the material appear "fresh" to your students.

In our last lesson, we talked about what it means to be holy. Today we're going to examine this a little further. How many of you like to get grade cards? How do you feel when you get lots of A's? What about C's? Now, what about F's? No, F's are not a good thing, because it usually means that we are struggling in a certain area of our learning. Maybe the subject is hard for us to understand, or maybe we're just not trying hard enough to understand it!

I wonder what kind of grade we would get if God handed out "Holiness Grade Cards." Would we receive an A, or not?

I want everyone to put on their thinking caps. *I'm going to wear mine, too, because holiness isn't just for kids. I need to work on my habits as well!* I'm will ask several questions throughout this lesson, but don't answer any of them aloud. They are simply to make us think.

- *Do I really try to live as Jesus would?* I know that it is impossible for me to be perfect, for only God is perfect. However, my goal should be to work at being Christ-like. Do I do this every day?
- *How do I act at school?* Am I a true Christian?

When we have the Holy Ghost, it means that God's Spirit lives *inside* of us! He goes *everywhere* with us. (If you have not yet received the Holy Ghost, He does not yet live in you, although He does know everything that you do.) Would God be interested in being our best friend if He were here on earth? He longs for us to be holy like Him! **Leviticus 19:2** says *"Ye shall be holy: for I the Lord your God am holy."* **(KJV)**

Definition of a Christian: *"A real disciple of Christ; one who believes in the truth of the Christian religion, and studies to follow the example, and obey the precepts, of Christ."*[31] (A precept is another word for teaching, or example.) We are to obey Christ's example and work to be like Him every single day. Let's look at a few areas, where a Christian may struggle, to see how we do on our "spiritual grade card."

Having disrespect for elders

Do we always treat adults with the respect that they deserve? We need to respect those who are in leadership; our parents or guardian, our teachers, our pastor, etc. There may be times when we want to joke with an adult; however, we need to be careful when, and how, we do this. It is okay to have fun, but we must remember that teasing them is not appropriate when it is accompanied with a disrespectful tone or manner. Even if an adult does not hold a leadership position in your life, you should still treat them with respect.

---

[31] Noah Webster's 1828 Dictionary of American English

- **(Isaiah 3:5 GW)** *"People will oppress each other, and everyone will oppress his neighbor. **The young will make fun of the old**, and common people will make fun of their superiors."*
- **(Leviticus 19:32 GW)** *"Show respect to the elderly, and honor older people. In this way you show respect for your God. I am the LORD."*
- **(Deuteronomy 5:16 CEV)** *"Respect your father and mother, and you will live a long and successful life in the land I am giving you."*
- **(Leviticus 19:3 GW)** *"Respect your mother and father."*

Rebellion

Do we always obey when we are told to do something? Or, do we ignore the person telling us what to do, thinking that maybe they'll forget what they said to us?

- **(Hebrews 13:17 CEV)** *"Obey your leaders and do what they say. They are watching over you, and they must answer to God. So don't make them sad as they do their work. Make them happy. Otherwise, they won't be able to help you at all."*
- **(1 Samuel 15:23 GW)** *"The sin of black magic is rebellion."*
- **(Psalm 103:12 GW)** *"As far as the east is from the west- that is how far he has removed our rebellious acts from himself."* ("He" is referring to God.)
- **(Psalm 51:3 GW)** *"I admit that I am rebellious. My sin is always in front of me."*

Did you listen to the scripture we just read? King David wrote it because He knew he had rebelled against God. Because he was constantly in repentance for wrongdoing, he is called the "man after God's own heart!"

Excluding others from friendship

Do we belong to a group of friends that excludes other people? This is called a "clique." Although someone may act differently than you, it is still not right to ignore him or her, or disassociate (remove) yourself from them.

- **(James 2:8-9 GW)** *"You are doing right if you obey this law from the highest authority: "Love your neighbor as you love yourself. If you favor one person over another, you're sinning, and this law convicts you of being disobedient."*
- **(Proverbs 18:24 KJV)** *"A man that hath friends must show himself friendly: and there is a friend that sticketh closer than a brother."*
- **(Proverbs 17:17a KJV)** *"A friend loveth at all times…"*
- **(Romans 12:10 GNT)** *"Love one another warmly as Christians, and be eager to show respect for one another."*

Gossip

Do we talk about others and say mean things about them when they can't hear us? Do we laugh at them for things that they do or say? When someone realizes that they are the subject of gossip, it creates a wound in their heart that, many times, only God can heal. We need to think about what we say before we say it. Does it build someone up, or make someone else feel badly?

- **(Proverbs 16:28 GNT)** *"Gossip is spread by wicked people; they stir up trouble and break up friendships."*
- **(Proverbs 20:19 GNT)** *"A gossip can never keep a secret. Stay away from people who talk too much."*
- **(Proverbs 26:20 GNT)** *"Without wood, a fire goes out; without gossip, quarreling stops."*
- **(Proverbs 11:13 CEV)** *"A gossip tells everything, but a true friend will keep a secret."*

Lying/Dishonesty

This one speaks for itself. Everyone knows what a lie is, and no one wants to be known as someone who tells one! Lying is also mentioned in Proverbs 6:19 as one of the things that the Lord hates.

- **(Proverbs 6:12 GW)** *"A good-for-nothing scoundrel is a person who has a dishonest mouth."*
- **(Proverbs 12:19 GW)** *"The word of truth lasts forever, but lies last only a moment."*
- **(1 John 2:4 CEV)** *"But if we claim to know him and don't obey him, we are lying and the truth isn't in our hearts."*
- **(Revelation 21:8 KJV)** *"But the fearful, and unbelieving, and abominable, and murderers, and whoremongers, and sorcerers, and idolaters, and all liars, shall have their part in the lake which burneth with fire and brimstone: which is the second death."*

Problems with temper; Teasing for spite

How do we act when we are with our brothers and sisters? And when we are with our friends at school? Do we tease or pick on others? Do we start arguments either because we think we are always right, or just because we like to upset other people for fun?

- **(Proverbs 29:22 GW)** *"An angry person stirs up a fight, and a hothead does much wrong."*
- **(Proverbs 20:3 GW)** *"Avoiding a quarrel is honorable. After all, any stubborn fool can start a fight."*
- **(Proverbs 25:28 GNT)** *"If you cannot control your anger, you are as helpless as a city without walls, open to attack."*
- **(Proverbs 15:18 CEV)** *"Losing your temper causes a lot of trouble, but staying calm settles arguments."*

A wise person is one who can walk away from an argument with a good attitude, not holding anything against the person who was angry with them.

Things Done in Secret

What do we mean when we say "things done in secret?" That means doing *anything* that you wouldn't want someone to know about! It could be a movie or television program that you watch, words that you say, books that you read, conversations that you have with others, music that you listen to, etc. Anything can be a "secret thing" if you are hiding it!

- **(Ecclesiastes 12:14 GW)** *"God will certainly judge everything that is done. This includes every **secret thing**, whether it is good or bad."*
- **(Mark 4:22 GW)** *"There is nothing hidden that will not be revealed. There is nothing kept **secret** that will not come to light."*
- **(Romans 2:16 GW)** *"This happens as they face the day when God, through Christ Jesus, will judge people's secret thoughts. He will use the Good News that I am spreading to make that judgment."*
- **(Jeremiah 23:24 GNT)** *"No one can hide where I cannot see them. Do you not know that I am everywhere in heaven and on earth?"*

God knows what we do, when we do it, and where we do it. We may be able to hide things from our parents or others, but we can *never* hide anything from Him!

We must do all that we can to avoid both outward and inward sins. We need to work constantly on our relationship with God. Prayer and Bible reading are both necessary for us to grow spiritually. A flower that does not receive water on a regular basis will wither away and die. A piece of fruit that is not eaten will eventually become spoiled. Our Christian walk is the same! If we do not have a steady diet of prayer and reading God's Word, our Holy Ghost will not be able to sustain (or keep) us when we go through

rough times. This causes us to be spiritually weak, which gives the devil the opportunity to tempt us with things that we would normally ignore.

(1 Peter 5:8 KJV) *"Be sober, be vigilant; because your adversary the devil, as a roaring lion, walketh about, seeking whom he may devour."*

Following Jesus every day is easy as long as He is our focus. It also gives us a hope!

Matthew 5:8 says, "Blessed are the pure in heart, for they shall see God." **(KJV) Romans 12:12** tells us, *"Be happy in your confidence, be patient in trouble, and pray continually."* **(GW)** Jesus gave us several promises in His Word that tell us He is looking forward to seeing us in Heaven! **John 14:1-3** says, *"Let not your heart be troubled: ye believe in God, believe also in me. In my Father's house are many mansions: if it were not so, I would have told you. I go to prepare a place for you. And if I go and prepare a place for you, I will come again, and receive you unto myself; that where I am, there ye may be also."* **(KJV)**

Let's take a moment to talk to Jesus. He will help us fix those things we struggle with, for He's just waiting on us to ask Him!

A photographer takes many pictures before he or she gets that "shot of a lifetime."

For those of you who have the Holy Ghost, have you ever asked God to give you a bigger prayer language? To give you new words to say? When we were babies, our parents taught us new words, which helped expand our vocabulary (the words that we speak and understand). God would love to do the same for us because He is our Heavenly Father!

Let's all take a minute to talk to Jesus and get His heavenly water flowing in our hearts!

(Add the following if there are children in attendance who do not have the Holy Ghost.)
God came to earth as a baby named Jesus because He wanted to be with us. He had created man, and wanted to be able to spend time with him. After He rose from the grave, He knew that He would not be able to stay on earth. So, God sent His Spirit down, which we call the Holy Ghost, or Holy Spirit. "Holy" means Godlike and a "spirit" is something that is within us, so the Holy Ghost is God's Spirit within us!

To repent is to make a change for the better. We feel bad about things we've done, and we want to change and not do them anymore! First, we must repent and ask Him to forgive us, because we can do and say mean things sometimes. To *repent* means to *feel pain, sorrow or regret for something done or spoken.*[32] Repentance is not just asking for forgiveness, it is deciding to make a change in your actions! Once we've asked Him to clean out our heart, He can move in, for God can't live in a dirty heart. Next, we need to be baptized. How? (*In the name of Jesus Christ*) Baptism washes away our sins **(Acts 2:38; 19:5)**. And then, the Bible says that you *will* receive the gift of the Holy Ghost! Did you know that you can receive the Holy Ghost before you're baptized? God isn't going to tell you that you have to wait!

We don't receive gifts because we earn them, but because people *love* us and want to give us something special. That's the way it is with the Holy Ghost! We haven't done anything to earn the Holy Ghost; God just wants us to have it because He loves us so much!

What happens when you are asking God for the Holy Ghost and He starts to move in your heart? Your lips may start feeling really funny! This is called "stammering lips." They feel funny, like when you've been out in the cold and they feel shivery. You will also begin hearing new words in your mind; they will be ones that you have never heard before. That is God speaking to you. **(Isaiah 28:11)** Your tongue will want to do funny things, and you must let it! That is Jesus trying to speak through you. It's important that you say the words! **(Acts 2:4, 38)** Why do you do this? Because that's the evidence (proof) that God is moving into your heart through the Holy Ghost! **(Acts 19:6)** When you start receiving the Holy Ghost, it is important not to stop yourself from speaking the new words heard in your mind. It's normal to feel the need to stop, but you don't want to; if you do, you will stop Jesus from moving into your heart.

Once you have received the Holy Ghost, you will feel different emotions, like love and joy. **(Isaiah 12:3; Habakkuk 3:18; Acts 13:52; Romans 14:17; 15:13; Galatians 5:22, 23)**

Teacher: Give all of your students a chance to pray. This would be a great time for either a new baby Christian to be born, or for the others to receive a refilling of God's precious Spirit.

---

[32] Noah Webster's 1828 Dictionary of American English

HOW DO I KEEP MY RIVER FLOWING?

Lesson suggestion: Whiteboard, markers. Also, wrap a small box with gift-wrap, as you will use it during the close of your lesson to example God's gift of the Holy Ghost. Another illustrative idea: obtain a glass pitcher and a large container of water. Slowly add water to the jar as you teach, signifying the constant power of His Spirit being poured into us every time we pray.

I have a question! How can we keep our river flowing? (Yes, our river!) Sometimes, when we've had the Holy Ghost for a while, we end up in a place of prayerlessness, meaning that we don't pray anymore; or, when we do pray, it's not with our whole heart. Just receiving the Holy Ghost isn't enough. We must learn to keep God's river flowing inside of us all the time, and this lesson is going to help you find out how to do just that!

Read John 4:5-14. The woman that Jesus met at the well was very lonely and sad. She had not been wise in the choices she had made concerning her life. Because of this, she did not have many friends in the city where she lived. Jesus knew that she was sad, and He really wanted to help her see that life could be different for her. Every day, this woman went alone to draw water from the well because she needed it for drinking, cooking, and washing. When she went there on this particular day, Jesus was sitting there waiting for her. He told her, "If you knew who I was, you'd be asking Me for a drink, and I would give you living water." She was confused! What did He mean? Could He really give her a water supply that would never run out? If He could, she wouldn't have to go to the well anymore! **(John 4:15 GW)** *"The woman told Jesus, "Sir, give me this water! Then I won't get thirsty or have to come here to get water."* As it was, she had to go when it was very hot outside, instead of in the early morning like the other women, because they were not nice to her. She always went later to avoid any gossip or arguments. However, Jesus wasn't talking about an actual water supply. He was talking about spiritual water!

The water of His Spirit flows inside of us and gives us life! **(John 4:14 GW)** *"But those who drink the water that I will give them will never become thirsty again. In fact, the water I will give them will become in them a spring that gushes up to eternal life."* He was trying to show the woman that if she would believe in Him, He would never leave her!

Once you receive the Holy Ghost, your spiritual well will always have water in it. However, it's up to you to decide how *full* you want your well to be! His living water is always there to quench, (take away) the thirsty feeling caused by the world. If you make a bad decision and do something you shouldn't, His living water will wash your soul clean when you repent and ask His forgiveness.

The woman at the well wanted physical water to keep her from ever being thirsty, from ever having to go to the well again. Instead, Jesus told her about something so much better: His spirit (His living water) that would cleanse her sadness, take away her loneliness, remove her pain, and replace sorrow with joy!

The Bible says, *"All have sinned."* **(Romans 3:23 KJV)** It also says, *"He is faithful and just to forgive us."* **(1 John 1:8-9 KJV)** If we tell Him of our sin, He will cleanse us! **1 John 2:5** says that He will make His love perfect in everyone who keeps His Word.

In order for our Holy Ghost to flow continually, we must pray and read our Bible daily. Praying in tongues is also important, and once a week is just not enough. We must use our prayer language often! Think about this:

- An artist draws many pictures before he or she creates a special project or famous masterpiece.
- An athlete must practice many hours to be good enough to play for a major league team.
- An Olympic gymnast practices and trains for hours every day to learn how to jump, flip, and balance. He or she has to know how, when, and why to do what they do.

HOW CAN I MAKE MY TIME WITH GOD EVEN BETTER?

Lesson suggestion: *Devotional Study Sheet (located in the Teacher's Toolbox)*

Have you ever wondered how you could learn as much about the Bible as your pastor, your parents, or your Sunday School teacher? Are there times when you are sitting in church listening to the minister preach or teach and think, "Wow, how did he find all of that in just one verse?"

2 Timothy 2:15 says, *"Do your best to present yourself to God as a tried-and-true worker who isn't ashamed to teach the word of truth correctly."* **(GW) Psalm 119:15** says, *"I will think on Your Commandments and have respect to Your ways."* **(MKJV)**

You see, we need to study God's Word! You might say, "But I don't know how to study the Bible! And, I don't have any of the study books that I need!" Everyone feels this way when they're just beginning to learn how to study the Bible.

In this lesson, we will show you how to study God's Word by using only the Bible and a notebook. You will find it to be very easy; it's called the devotional method. There are just four steps to follow! *(Teacher: work through a scripture example as you teach the following.)*

1. **Read.**
   - *Choose a verse that grabs your attention*; this is what you are going to study. It should be something that will impact (change) you somehow."
   - Read the verse(s); then, write the scripture in your notebook.

2. **Pray.**
   - *Pray that God will help you to understand what you are reading.* Without His help, you may learn something about the Bible, but it will never make it into your heart. Write what you prayed into your notebook.

3. **Think about it (meditate).**
   - *To meditate means to think about something deeply. Write down your thoughts.* What comes to mind when you read the verse? You may need to read it several times. Listen to what God is trying to say; then, write your thoughts in your notebook. If it is difficult to understand what the verse is saying, ask your parent or teacher.

4. **How can you use the verse (apply it to your life)?**
   - *How are you going to use what God has said to you through His Word?* This is the imaginary glue that makes the verse "stick" in your mind! This is where you decide how you are going to change your life to match the Bible. Write this in your notebook.

5. **Memorize the verse.**
   - *Work to memorize the verse that you are studying Practice saying it to yourself, then to someone else; this will help you commit to memory.* It will help to fully write the verse(s) out in your notebook.

You have just studied your Bible! Was it as hard as what you thought it would be? This is where you can begin to make your relationship with God even bigger than it is now. Everyone needs to learn how to study His Word, because it's one of the ways that Jesus speaks to us. *(Teacher: Pass out the Devotional Study Sheets. Set a turn-in deadline to ensure that you see the results.)*

BECOMING A JOURNALIST FOR JESUS

Lesson suggestion: *This lesson is recommended for ages 8 and up. Buy a small, inexpensive notebook for each student. Specify that this is to be used solely for their prayer time (not to draw or doodle in during church services or playtime), and that they should respect it as such.*

During this lesson, we will learn how to become a *Journalist for Jesus.* You're probably wondering what that means, aren't you? The dictionary says that a *journalist* is *"the writer of a journal or diary."*[33] A *journal* is *"A diary; an account of daily transactions and events."*[34]

You might think that a journal is only for girls, something in which they write their secrets about life, friends, and things like that. Others might think it's only important for people who go on long trips, like captains on ships keeping track of their voyages, or explorers and excavators who make amazing discoveries. It's likely that that you have read from the journals of important people at school. "So why do we need to keep a journal?" you ask. You probably figure that your life is not that interesting; it may even sound sort of silly to you. It's not as if we make trips to the moon or have discovered some new invention that would change the world! Why should *we* have a journal?

Because we serve a very wonderful and loving God, we should keep a journal for several special and important reasons. *(Have the children write the following two points in the front of their notebook. This will serve to remind them of their purpose.)*

We need to write down when He speaks to us. The Lord spoke to Paul. **(Acts 18:9, 10 CEV)** *"One night, Paul had a vision, and in it the Lord said, 'Don't be afraid to keep on preaching. Don't stop! I am with you, and you won't be harmed. Many people in this city belong to me.'"*

We need to record special things that we see or hear Him do, or things that He does for us! (Jonah 2:10 KJV) *"So the LORD spoke to the fish, and it vomited Jonah onto dry land."* Wouldn't that be an experience to remember? **(Exodus 8:5 GW)** *"Then the LORD said to Moses, "Tell Aaron, 'Hold your staff over the rivers, canals, and ponds. This will bring frogs onto the land.'"*

You may not think that you are as important as Philip or Paul, and your life may not be as exciting as Jonah's or Moses'! But, can you think of something wonderful that God has done for you? When has He healed you? What about the very instant that you *knew* He loved you? How did you feel? How did you feel just after you received the Holy Ghost? How did you feel after you talked to someone about Jesus for the first time? What emotions do you experience when He answers one of your prayers?

These are all very important events in our walk with God, and we need to *remember* them! Each one can be a reminder to us when we become discouraged and sad. They are a testimony of His goodness and His love toward us! A journal keeps us in touch with our relationship with Him.

A journal is a very private thing between you and Jesus, sort of like a conversation between you and Him in writing. You are never too young to start one! You can write down your thoughts, your experiences, and your prayers. You can copy a scripture that helps you, either when you are having a rough time, or you are very happy and want to worship Him. God's Word is a light for us at all times!

The Bible says, *"Sing unto the LORD, O ye saints of his, and give thanks at the remembrance of his holiness."* **(Psalm 30:4 KJV)**

(John 14:26 KJV) *"But the Comforter, which is the Holy Ghost, whom the Father will send in my name, he shall teach you all things, and bring all things to your remembrance, whatsoever I have said unto you."*

---

[33] Noah Webster's 1828 Dictionary of American English
[34] Noah Webster's 1828 Dictionary of American English

You should also write down what God says to you during prayer. Our lives are very busy and sometimes, it is hard to remember important things that happen. However, we've learned that we should learn to be still and quiet in His presence. That way, we will be able to hear when God speaks to us, for when He does, it is *always* important. He loves to encourage us, and He will speak promises to you. If you write them down, they are there for you to read later during a time of discouragement. Reading God's promises would help you feel so much better!

The Bible says to remember what He has done! *"Our LORD, I will remember the things you have done, your miracles of long ago."* **(Psalms 77:11 CEV)**

Let's enjoy this new way to get to know God better. I'm looking forward to seeing you grow in your relationship with God as you remember what He does for you!

(YOU + ME) + WORKING TOGETHER = UNITY

Lesson suggestion: A small puzzle that can be completed in 1-2 minutes. Explain the object lesson to your student helpers prior to the start of class.

Today we're going to learn about a very important concept (or idea). It's called "unity."

What is unity?

The dictionary says that the word "unity" simply means "oneness" or "not being multiple." This does not mean that we should act like robots that don't have a mind, or the ability to make choices; it simply means that there is one purpose (or reason) for existing. For example, would you be alive if your heart and your lungs decided that they both had the same job? No! They each have their own function, but they have the same purpose: to keep you alive. If they didn't work together, you wouldn't live very long!

Why is unity important?

Think about putting together a puzzle. Could you put it together more quickly by yourself, or with some friends helping you? Let's have a demonstration and see!

Demonstration (time the exercise each time, giving 1-2 minutes to complete the puzzle):
1. *Choose a child to put the simple puzzle together by itself.*
2. *Have two children work on the same puzzle; the second person should take pieces away from the puzzle, rather than add to it.*
3. *Have two children work on the same puzzle in unity.*

Did you notice how much faster the last team finished the puzzle? I have a question. Could *one person* defeat your favorite ball team? No, they would lose miserably. Why? Because unity (people working together) brings energy and excitement! Teamwork is powerful when everyone works together towards the same goal, whether it is to win a ball game, complete a school project, sing a special song as a group, etc.

Does the Bible have any examples of unity?

In **Genesis 11:1-9**, we learn about the Tower of Babel. The people of that day would have built a great tower if God had not chosen to confuse them! Let's look at what the Bible says in **Genesis 11:6**. *"The Lord said, "Behold, they are one people, and they have all one language; and this is only the beginning of what they will do; and nothing that they propose to do will now be impossible for them."* **(RSV)** God placed within us the ability to accomplish *anything we can imagine* through the power of unity. The people working on the tower were not on God's team. Their shared goal was to build a tower to Heaven, and God knew that it was not a good goal for them to have.

In **1 Samuel 14:6-7, 13-14**, we read how Jonathan and his armor bearer took on twenty soldiers and won! The unity of these two men fighting together, with God on their side, caused the Philistines to be afraid of the Israelites, and the men with Saul and Jonathon ending up winning the battle!

Acts 2 talks about the Day of Pentecost. On that particular day, 120 people had the same goal. Each person wanted the Comforter that Jesus had promised to send when He went to Heaven. Because they were focused on the same goal, the Church was born that day! In **Acts 2:1**, the Bible says that they were in "one accord" or "one mind." This could also be explained as being "unanimous." "Unanimous" means "common," or "to be in agreement." If I asked a question and all of you had the same answer, it would mean that you answered "unanimously."

Does the Bible have any advice regarding unity?

John 13:34-35 tells us to love one another. Did you know that the more you love someone, the more you want him or her to do well, or be happy? Without love, it is almost impossible to have unity. When others see us loving each other, they will know that we are Jesus' disciples, and will learn from our example.

In **1 Corinthians 1:10**, Paul was encouraging the church in Corinth to be unified. You see, they could not all meet in one building because there were too many people. Instead, they met in homes and each group had its own leader, or preacher. Some liked "their preacher" better than they liked the others, and this caused them to develop cliques *(a clique is a group of people that is friendly only with each other, excluding other people)*. Arguing over things like that had become more important than telling other people about Jesus. When we all work to reach the same goal, we will want what is best for the whole group, and we will be less concerned with ourselves.

Were the first Christians unified?

Read Acts 4:32-37. The Roman government had been persecuting the Christians and as a result, many had lost their homes. Because of this, the believers in Jerusalem sold their own properties and gave the money to the Apostles; they wanted to be sure that everyone had food and shelter. This happened because the people were in complete agreement (or unity). Now, we are not talking about a small church! This group of believers began with at least 8,000 men as members, not even counting the women and kids! If there were four people to a family, this verse could be describing about 32,000 people. Can you imagine what 32,000 people could do if they were working together?

Here we also find the first mention of Satan trying to destroy the unity of the church. **Read Acts 5:1-10**. God was very protective of the unity that the early Christians were experiencing. Can you imagine what God could do if **we** became unified? Just think of what God could do if we all had the same goal: to become the best follower of Christ that we can! Let's read **Acts 5:12-15** to see what happened after God removed the people who were not acting in unity.

Can you imagine walking with God so closely that people are healed by your shadow? That would truly be so wonderful, to be so close to God that He trusted you or me enough to share a gift of healing like that with us! Being one with Jesus is something that we should work towards each and every day.

DISOBEDIENCE VS. OBEDIENCE:
How does God view them?

Lesson suggestion: Whiteboard, markers.

We are often told that we are should obey our parents. *"Children, obey your parents in the Lord, for this is right. Honor your father and mother (which is the first commandment with a promise), so that it may be well with you, and that you may live long on the earth."* **(Ephesians 6:1-3 MKJV) (Exodus 20:12)** When we don't, they almost always tell us that we have been disobedient. Parents have the job of raising their kids and teaching them to do the right thing, be a good person, be responsible, etc. So, when we disobey, it's their God-given job to teach us right from wrong. **(Deuteronomy 11:18-21)** *"My child, listen when your father corrects you. Don't neglect your mother's instruction."* **(Proverbs 1:8 NLT)**

Is obedience as important to God as it is to our parents? Let's see!

Obedience example #1

Read Daniel 3:1-23 aloud. King Nebuchadnezzar built a statue; then, he made a law requiring all of the people in the land of Babylon to worship it. There were three Jews, Shadrach, Meshach, and Abednego, who refused to worship the statue because they worshipped the one true God, Jehovah. They refused to do the things that the king wanted them to do, and it made him very angry!

The king commanded that the furnace be heated seven times hotter than normal, then they threw the three men into the furnace! Because Shadrach, Meshach, and Abednego were faithful to God and obeyed the laws that He had given the Jews, God took care of them and saved them from the furnace! **Read Daniel 3:24-30.** Can you imagine the look on the king's face when he saw the fourth person in the fire? That is an amazing miracle!

Obedience Example #2

Read Genesis 6:8-22 aloud. God looked upon the earth and saw the people that He had created doing many evil things. He repented that He had made them and decided to destroy every living thing. But, God also saw Noah, who was a good man who served the Lord with all of his heart. This pleased God and made Him decide to give Noah a special job, which meant that he and his family would all be saved!

God asked Noah to build a very large boat called an ark, then gave him specific directions explaining how Noah was to build it. It took Noah and his sons more than 30 years to build the ark. Wow! That's a long time, isn't it? Not only did it take him such a long time to build the ark, he was also made fun of the whole time he was working! People teased and made fun of Noah as he preached about the water that God would send down to the earth in the form of a flood. You see, it had never rained! The Lord caused dew to come each morning; there were also rivers and streams that the people pulled water from for drinking, bathing, and doing other things. No one had ever experienced a rainstorm, so they didn't believe it would really happen. Now, think about this. <u>Noah had never seen it rain.</u> He probably didn't really even understand the concept of rain. He could have easily given up on the huge project God had given him. After all, it took him many, many years. He was made fun of by everyone! It would have been very easy to stop working on the ark. But, he didn't, and because he trusted God and obeyed Him, his family was saved! God used Noah to save many of the kinds of animals that we enjoy seeing today. But do you know what is most important? If Noah had not obeyed, we would not even be here right now! God destroyed everything else on the earth; only those in the ark were saved.

Disobedience example #1

Read 2 Samuel 6:1-3 aloud. David went to get the Ark of the Covenant from Abinadab's house. The men that went with him set the ark upon a new cart, which was in direct disobedience to what God had said to do! Rather, it was to be carried by the sons of Kohath (who was a son of Levi, the son of Jacob, whose descendants, or relatives, were chosen for the priesthood). Their job was to "carry" the holy things of the tabernacle.

Read 2 Samuel 6:6-7 aloud. Uzzah put forth his hand to steady the ark and died! His death was actually a result of God's displeasure at David's disobedience. Remember: how were they supposed to transport the ark, and how did David have the men do it? Uzzah violated God's holiness by touching the ark! King David must have learned his lesson, because when he moved the ark the second time, he did it the right way! Just think. If he had obeyed the first time, Uzzah wouldn't have died. That is a hard way to learn a lesson, isn't it?

Disobedience example #2

Read Numbers 20:2, 6-8 aloud. The Israelites were thirsty and needed water, so God told Moses to speak to the rock and He would supply what they needed. But, Moses was angry with the people because of their complaining, so he hit the rock with his rod instead. That doesn't sound like a really awful thing, does it? But, did you know that because Moses disobeyed God, neither he nor Aaron was allowed to go to the Promised Land? They both died while still in the wilderness. The Bible does not explain why Aaron was punished along with Moses, but it is clear that sometimes, our disobedience can hurt other people as well.

We have learned that there are consequences when we disobey. David disobeyed and Uzzah died. Moses and Aaron disobeyed, and they were not allowed to enter the Promised Land. Regardless of what we do, we are accountable for our actions. We may ask forgiveness when we disobey, but this doesn't mean that our punishment will be taken away! David, Moses, and Aaron were most likely very sorry for what they had done, but God did not change (or remove) their punishment. *"For the wages of sin is death; but the gift of God is eternal life through Jesus Christ our Lord."* **(Romans 6:23 KJV)**

However, just as there are consequences for disobedience, there are also rewards when we obey and do as we should. Just as Shadrach, Meshach, and Abednego were spared from the fiery furnace, and Noah and his family were saved, I'm sure that you have also been rewarded for your obedience. **(Ephesians 6:1-2)**

Because Adam chose to sin, we were born into sin, too. But when Jesus came to earth, we were given a chance to redeem ourselves through Him. *"Yes, Adam's one sin brings condemnation for everyone, but Christ's one act of righteousness brings a right relationship with God and new life for everyone. Because one person disobeyed God, many became sinners. But because one other person obeyed God, many will be made righteous."* **(Romans 5:18-19 NLT)**

Our reward for obeying God's commandments regarding salvation is that we will be able to live with Him in Heaven someday. Once we have repented, been baptized, and received the Holy Ghost, it is up to us to do what is right. When we obey what the Word of God says, we will always win! **Read Revelation 22:12-14 aloud.**

HAVING HONOR AND RESPECT FOR OTHERS

Lesson suggestion: Whiteboard, markers.

Honor: "special esteem or respect"

- **Respect:** We show respect when we show consideration or appreciation for someone else.
- **Esteem:** Esteem is to have, or show, respect.

We have often heard that we should honor and respect our parents, but did you also know that the Bible is very explicit (or plainspoken) about this? There are many scriptures that talk about obeying, honoring, and respecting your parents! **Read Exodus 20:12** (Commandment #5 of the Ten Commandments). **(Proverbs 1:8; Matthew 19:19; Ephesians 6:1-3)**

To honor your parents is to respect, or hold esteem for, them. God has given your parents the responsibility of raising you. This includes teaching you and exposing you to many things so that you will have knowledge, both physically and spiritually. *"My son, obey the command of your father, and do not disregard the teachings of your mother."* **(Proverbs 6:20 GW)**

Not only are you to respect your parents, but you should respect other adults, too (Teachers at both school and church, grandparents, adults at church, guardians, etc.) *"Remember your leaders who have spoken God's word to you. Think about how their lives turned out, and imitate their faith."* **(Hebrews 13:7 GW)**

Respecting your teachers, your friends, and your family probably sounds like a big job. When you choose to act a certain way all of the time, it is called having a mindset (a certain way of thinking). This means that you've made up your mind, and you're not changing it for anything or anyone!

Read Hebrews 12:1 and 2 Peter 1:5-10. As a Christian, we should have the following fruits evident in our lives.

Temperance:	Moderation or self-restraint **(2 Peter 1:6)**
Patience:	Understanding; tolerance **(2 Peter 1:6)**
Godliness:	Having the nature of God **(1 Timothy 6:6)**
Brotherly kindness:	Showing kindness, good will to others **(Ephesians 4:32)**
Charity (Love):	A feeling of affection **(1 Corinthians 13:13)**

Because we are human, we must continually work on ourselves (our attitudes and actions). If the attributes (qualities or characteristics) mentioned in **2 Peter 1:5** are at work in our lives, it will be easier to respect others!

Discussion time: To whom do you think you could show more respect? How could you do this? Jesus is always ready to help you; you just need to ask Him!

INTEGRITY:
What Is It, and Do I Have to Have It?

Lesson suggestion: Whiteboard, markers. This lesson contains less verbiage in order to allow more time for scripture reading, as the topic is one that is extremely important and needs full Biblical understanding.

Today's lesson is about integrity. A person who continues doing what they believe is right, even when faced with difficult circumstances, is said to have integrity. Do you think it is necessary to have integrity in order to walk with Jesus? (Yes, it is necessary!) **[Integrity: Firm adherence to a code or standard of values.[35]]**

We're going to study a few different people from the Bible to find out whether or not they acted with integrity.

When a king won a battle, he would often take captives from the losing country back to where he lived; those captives would then become slaves for whatever job the king needed them to do. The man in this story, King Nebuchadnezzar, conquered the Jews who lived in the land of Judah. From those captives, he chose young men who were very healthy, strong, smart, and handsome; then, he took them back to his country, Babylon. The king's plan was to change them so that they would act like Babylonians instead of Jews. He captured four young men who ended up being a part of several very special Bible stories. Each one tells how these men acted with integrity in the midst of situations that they faced. They were *Daniel* (Belteshazzar), Hananiah (*Shadrach*), Mishael (*Meshach*), and Azariah (*Abednego*). *(The first name for each was their given Jewish name; the second is the Babylonian name given to them by King Nebuchadnezzar. During this lesson, we will use the names Daniel, Shadrach, Meshach, and Abednego as they are referred to in the particular instances discussed in this lesson.)*

We said that there are several special Bible stories that involve these men. Let's get started and find out what they are!

As we said before, Daniel, Shadrach, Meshach, and Abednego were captured and taken to Babylon, where they began to have problems right away!

Problem #1

The Babylonians prepared their foods differently than the Jews. Many times, they would eat meat that Jews were not allowed to eat, such as pork. They would also offer their meat to idols as an offering before serving it. Daniel, Shadrach, Meshach, and Abednego knew that by eating the King's meat, they would be breaking a Jewish law. Rather than go against what they believed, they made an agreement with one of the King's workers. **Read Daniel 1:8-14 aloud.**

Read Daniel 1:15-16 aloud. Instead of having to eat the King's meat and drink his wine, they were given permission to eat vegetables and drink water for ten days. It was a "test" by their caretaker to see if their idea would really work or not!

Because they chose to follow what they believed, God helped them! The Bible says that He gave them knowledge and skill, and they were set above (or given higher responsibility) all of the others because they did what they knew was right! If they had eaten the king's meat, they would have become spiritually sick (meaning that it would have affected their walk with God, as they would have chosen to ignore the food laws that God had put in place for the Jews).

Daniel was given a very special job working with the king, and Shadrach, Meshach, and Abednego were given important jobs in the government of Babylon.

---

[35] Webster's II New Riverside Dictionary, pg. 634.

Problem #2

The Babylonians worshipped many different idols. This problem became a very big one for Shadrach, Meshach, and Abednego. King Nebuchadnezzar had his workers create a huge statue. When it was finished, the king declared a worship day and gathered all of the people. He had one easy rule: "When you hear the music, bow to my statue! If you don't, I'll throw you into my fiery furnace!" That sounds easy enough, right? Wrong!

Shadrach, Meshach, and Abednego knew that bowing and worshipping the king's idol was wrong. They worshipped the one true God of Israel. So, when the music played, everyone bowed except them! The king became very angry. He gave them a second chance, but they still wouldn't bow down and worship his statue. **Read Daniel 3:16-23 aloud.**

It sounds like Shadrach, Meshach, and Abednego are in big trouble, doesn't it? Well, maybe not! **Read Daniel 3:24-30 aloud.**

Because Shadrach, Meshach, and Abednego did what they knew was right by not worshipping the King's idol, an entire nation learned about the one true God!

Discussion:

- When have you acted with integrity?
- When *should* you act with integrity?

There is another man in the Bible who acted with integrity; his name was Paul: **Read 2 Corinthians 11:23-31 aloud.**

The Apostle Paul suffered many persecutions because of his ministry and belief in God. He could have easily decided that the pain and cost was too much! He could have stopped preaching and went into hiding so that he could not be found. But did he? No! He continued to teach, preach, and pastor many churches until he was finally put in prison and eventually beheaded (punished by having his head removed).

How many of us would have enough integrity to live as Paul did? What about Shadrach, Meshach, and Abednego? That's a hard question, and something that we really need to consider. We may never be subjected to persecution as Paul was, or have to stand up for our faith like Shadrach, Meshach, and Abednego, but we need to be sure that our relationship with God is strong enough to help us withstand such things if necessary.

WHAT KIND OF EXAMPLE ARE YOU?

Lesson suggestion: Whiteboard, markers

We are often told to be a good example. What is an example, and why do we need to work at being a good one? Why do we even have to be an example at all? I'm sure we've all asked these questions at least once.

You are an example either when you represent a group, or when others watch to see what you do (including how you treat others). We are all examples, whether or not we want to be one!

Let's look at what some famous people have said about being an example:

- *"What you do speaks so loudly that I cannot hear what you say." - Ralph Waldo Emerson*
- *"Nothing preaches better than the act." - Benjamin Franklin*

Bad examples

(2 Kings 15:17-18 GNT) *"In the thirty-ninth year of the reign of King Uzziah of Judah, Menahem son of Gadi became king of Israel, and he ruled in Samaria for ten years. He sinned against the Lord, for until the day of his death he followed the wicked example of King Jeroboam son of Nebat, who led Israel into sin."*

(2 Chronicles 36:14 GNT) *"In addition, the leaders of Judah, the priests, and the people followed the sinful example of the nations around them in worshiping idols, and so they defiled the Temple, which the Lord himself had made holy."*

- Many kings worshiped idols (statues made by men), choosing to completely forget about God.
- The priests (men who were supposed to be holy and teach the people about God) also worshipped idols and were very bad examples to the people.

Good examples

(2 Kings 18:3-6 GNT) *"Following the example of his ancestor King David, he did what was pleasing to the Lord. He destroyed the pagan places of worship, broke the stone pillars, and cut down the images of the goddess Asherah. He also broke in pieces the bronze snake that Moses had made, which was called Nehushtan. Up to that time the people of Israel had burned incense in its honor. Hezekiah trusted in the Lord, the God of Israel; Judah never had another king like him, either before or after his time. He was faithful to the Lord and never disobeyed him, but carefully kept all the commands that the Lord had given Moses."*

- King Hezekiah destroyed the places that were used to worship idols (gods made by man).
- He trusted in the Lord, was faithful, and never disobeyed Him.

(2 Kings 22:1-2 GNT) *"Josiah was eight years old when he became king of Judah, and he ruled in Jerusalem for thirty-one years. His mother was Jedidah, the daughter of Adaiah from the town of Bozkath. Josiah did what was pleasing to the Lord; he followed the example of his ancestor King David, strictly obeying all the laws of God."*

- King Josiah obeyed all of the laws of God, just as King David had done. He was a good example to the people of Judah.

What kind of example are you? At different times throughout our lives, we will be both a good or bad example to others. *(Teacher: Insert a personal example to help explain this concept).* In this lesson, we are choosing to focus on the spiritual example that we are setting. "Are you a good example of a Christian?" When people are around you, what do they see?

The Apostle Paul tried to be a good example at all times. **(Acts 20:35)** You might ask, "How can I be a good example?" Read the following scriptures: **(Proverbs 2:20; 3:31-32; 20:7; Isaiah 51:1; 1 Timothy 4:11-12)**

If we are always mad or sad, others will not be interested in meeting our Jesus. But if we are happy and kind, people will want to know about Him! It isn't possible to keep from being an example, because someone is always watching how you live. It may be a little brother or sister, a friend, or maybe even a parent. Jesus can use your example (or witness) to reach someone who doesn't know Him!

I'M CALLED TO BE A SOULWINNER!

Lesson suggestion: *Props (see examples below): Cereal box, book, toy, or whatever fits with your idea of a "commercial" that would be enticing to a child.*

Today's lesson is about a very important subject: soulwinning! Does anyone know what it means to be a soulwinner? *(Student feedback)*

Mr. Webster's dictionary says that a soul is *"that part of man which enables him to think and reason."* [36] He also refers to the soul *as "a human being, or a person."* [37] So, we could say that the soul is the part of us that helps us think and reason! Who can help me with the definition of "winner?" Yes, it is "someone who wins!"

So, what would be the definition of a soulwinner? (S*tudent feedback)* A soulwinner is someone who wins over the thinking (or reasoning) of another person. What does that mean, and how can we do that?

I have a couple of examples that will help us better understand this. Let's talk about them!

Commercials *(use whatever props will work here, such as cereal boxes, magazine ads, etc.)*

Commercials work to win over our thinking! What types of commercials have you heard, read, or seen? *(Ask for feedback)* Does the commercial for your favorite cereal ever tell you that it will get soggy after just a few minutes? No; it only talks about how good it tastes!

Yourself

How many of you have ever tried to convince your mom or dad that you really need that new toy? A new dress? A new pair of shoes? A new racecar track? When you want something, you do whatever you can to convince your parents that you just have to have it!

Now that you have the idea, let's talk about soulwinning again. Remember, you are a soulwinner when you win over the thinking of another person.

What would be our goal as a soulwinner? To help someone see their need for God in their life.

How do we do this? Show them His love. Live a consistent Christian life in front of them.

Whom can we win to Jesus? (Ask for feedback: school friends, next-door neighbors, etc.)

Let's look at a few examples of men who witnessed to others about Jesus.

Philip

Read Acts 8:26-39 Philip was an apostle of Jesus Christ. One day, the Lord sent him into the desert specifically to meet a man who was reading the scriptures; the man did not understand what he was reading and needed someone to help him. Philip told the man all about Jesus and the good things that had happened because of Him. Philip's testimony was so life-changing to the man that he immediately wanted to be baptized!

Saul, whose name was later changed to Paul

When Saul was converted on the road to Damascus, God spoke to him and said, *"Stand up! I have appeared to you for a reason. I'm appointing you to be a servant and witness of what you have seen and of what I will show you. I will rescue you from the Jewish people and from the non-Jewish people*

---

[36] Noah Webster's 1828 Dictionary of American English
[37] Noah Webster's 1828 Dictionary of American English

to whom I am sending you. You will open their eyes and turn them from darkness to light and from Satan's control to God's. Then they will receive forgiveness for their sins and a share among God's people who are made holy by believing in me." **(Acts 26:16-18 GW)** Paul was also told in **Acts 22:15**, *"For thou shalt be his witness unto all men of what thou hast seen and heard."* **(KJV)**

Paul's choice to follow Jesus was a great testimony to other people! Because he had done so many things to hurt the Christians before his conversion, everyone knew that his experience had to be real. Many people chose to live for God because of the changes that they saw happen in Paul's life.

Peter

Peter preached on the day of Pentecost and told the people what had happened in the Upper Room. **(Acts 2:37-29)** *"Now when they heard this, they were pricked in their heart, and said unto Peter and to the rest of the apostles, Men and brethren, what shall we do? Then Peter said unto them, Repent, and be baptized every one of you in the name of Jesus Christ for the remission of sins, and ye shall receive the gift of the Holy Ghost. For the promise is unto you, and to your children, and to all that are afar off, even as many as the Lord our God shall call."* **(KJV)**

The people that heard Peter preach on the day of Pentecost knew that he was not educated. The way that he spoke proved that he was just a simple man, because he did not use fancy or "big" words. As a matter of fact, nearly all of the people who were in the Upper Room were just like Peter. Because they all spoke in many languages – languages that the people around them understood and spoke – those listening understood that something supernatural and wonderful had just taken place. God gave every person in the Upper Room an important testimony that they were able to share with everyone around them!

Luke 19:10 says, *"For the Son of man is come to seek and to save that which was lost."* **(KJV)** Who are lost? Those who don't yet know Jesus!

Now, how can we be soulwinners for Him? *(Student feedback: tell others about Jesus, act like Jesus, have good attitudes and actions, etc.)*

The very first step to being a soulwinner is to love others. Jesus can help us do that! **1 Corinthians 13:4-8a** says, *"Love is kind and patient, never jealous, boastful, proud, or rude. Love isn't selfish or quick tempered. It doesn't keep a record of wrongs that others do. Love rejoices in the truth, but not in evil. Love is always supportive, loyal, hopeful, and trusting. Love never fails!"* **(CEV)**

Secondly, we need to tell others about Jesus. People who have received the Holy Ghost have a wonderful gift to share, but how will they know about it unless we tell them? **(1 Peter 3:15)** *"Honor Christ and let him be the Lord of your life. Always be ready to give an answer when someone asks you about your hope."* **(CEV)**

God does not expect you to be perfect; He simply wants you to do your best. When we work hard to be like Jesus, others notice, and it makes them want to be around us more. Then, we have a chance to be their friend and tell them about Him.

WOULD JESUS PLAY WITH MY FRIENDS?

Lesson suggestion: Whiteboard, markers.

We have probably heard our parents or guardian say, "Please choose your friends wisely." They are concerned about those with whom we choose to play and spend our time. Why is this so important?

There are many types of people in the world; therefore, there are many types of friends available to us. How are we supposed to choose our friends wisely? What should they be like? How can we know if they're the right person to have as a friend?

The Bible talks about many different friendships. Let's look at a few examples to see if these people made either good or bad choices when choosing their friends.

David and Jonathan: Read 1 Samuel 18:1-4

David and Jonathan truly were good friends. When Jonathan's father, King Saul, was trying to kill David, Jonathan protected him! He looked after David and loved him like a brother. Even after David had to leave, and he and Jonathan could no longer spend time with one another, neither one ever forgot their special friendship.

Samson and Delilah

Samson loved a woman that was not of his people. She was a Philistine, and her people did not serve the One True God. Instead, they worshipped idols. Also, their countries were constantly at war with one another; yet, Samson chose to love Delilah anyway. Maybe she really did consider Samson to be a good friend in the beginning. But then, the leaders of the Philistines came and offered her money to help them capture him. She just had to help them figure out the source of Samson's strength because they couldn't figure it out by themselves. They had to trick him somehow! Evidently, Delilah loved money more than she loved Samson, because she was more than happy to help those bad men learn his secret! Samson told her three different lies before he finally told her the truth about his strength. Then, when he finally did tell her the true source of his strength, she betrayed him to the Philistine men who wanted to capture him! Something about this just doesn't make sense: Samson obviously knew that something was wrong. Why would she care so much about where his strength came from? Wasn't Samson smart enough to know that Delilah was not a good person? Since he also told her lies, it was obvious that Samson's relationship with God wasn't right; he had allowed bad habits into his life, which caused him to make wrong choices. **Read Judges 16:15-20.** When the Philistines came to capture Samson, he did not even realize God had left him. That is a terrible thing.

Do our friends make us forget about Jesus? Do they talk about things they shouldn't, or say bad words? Do they do things that we know are not right? If they do, do we try to stop them, or are we afraid that they'll laugh at us if we say anything?

Make two lists on the Whiteboard:

List 1: qualities the children desire in a friend
List 2: qualities that they would not choose in a friend

Let's ask ourselves a question. Would Jesus play with our friends? Would He want to spend time with them? Would He want to go to their house? Would He want to listen to their music? Would He want to listen to them talk? Would He watch their TV shows? Would He read their books or magazines, or play their video games?

Now, ask yourself this question, but don't answer it out loud. Just think about it in your mind. Do you have any friends with whom Jesus wouldn't want to play? If you answered "Yes" in your mind, what can you do to fix the situation so that Jesus would want to play with them? (Suggestion: have a group discussion about ways that the children can be good examples to friends who do not know Jesus.)

Sometimes, we know that our friends are doing wrong things, but we're not able to help them see the need for change. When this happens, it is probably a good idea to find new friends that compliment who we are, or who we *want* to be. This doesn't mean that we shouldn't be kind, or show love, to people who don't love Jesus! We should always be a witness. However, there are scriptures in the Bible that talk about choosing friends wisely. **Read Proverbs 24:1 and Philippians 2:1-2.**

Jesus is always willing to help us make wise choices. We just need to ask Him!

PART II

Biblical Concepts and Doctrine

Train up a child in the way he should go: and when he is old, he will not depart from it.

(Proverbs 22:6 KJV)

TWO PLANS FOR YOUR LIFE

Lesson suggestion: Whiteboard, markers.

Have you ever heard someone say, "You can't have it both ways?" This phrase usually means that a person needs to make a choice. In the Bible, God clearly explains the plan that He has put in place for each one of His children. However, someone else is also interested in you! It is important that we understand what the Bible says so that we can make wise choices.

God had become upset with things that some of the Christians had been doing. Because of this, he had the Apostle John write letters to seven different churches. Listen to what God said to the church of Laodicea: *"I have knowledge of your works, that you are not cold or warm: it would be better if you were cold or warm. So because you are not one thing or the other, I will have no more to do with you."* **(Revelations 3:15, 16 BBE)**

The Christians in Laodicea weren't openly sinning (or doing bad things). However, they were only going through the motions of serving God. They had lost their love for Him, so they had stopped seeking to grow in their relationship with Him. Because of this, God was no longer going to try to work on His part of the relationship, too.

While Jesus was on earth, He had some very honest and plain things to say; He wanted us to understand something very important: Satan is interested in destroying our relationship. He will do all that he can to make God seem unimportant and unnecessary to us. **(Matthew 6:24 GW)** *"No one can serve two masters. He will hate the first master and love the second, or he will be devoted to the first and despise the second. You cannot serve God and wealth."* The last sentence said, "You cannot serve God and wealth." Why would Jesus say that?

Satan's goal is to distract us with life. He knows that if he can get us to believe that "things" will make us happy, it will distract us from our relationship with God. Many people who have successful jobs, and make lots of money, end up "serving" their job. They work long hours at the office and spend most of their time making sure that their paycheck gets bigger and bigger. Money becomes their idol. This doesn't mean that money is a bad thing. It simply means that we must keep our thoughts about it in the right place, and not make it a "god" in our lives.

It is impossible for us to obey two different bosses at the same time. Have you ever been in a situation where your mom asked you to do one thing; then, your dad told you to do something else? They didn't mean to confuse you; they just didn't know that you had already been given something else to do! Just as it would be impossible to complete two chores at the very same time, it is impossible to satisfy your flesh (do what *you* want to do) and please God.

(Matthew 7:13-14 GW) *"Enter through the narrow gate because the gate and road that lead to destruction are wide. Many enter through the wide gate. But the narrow gate and the road that lead to life are full of trouble. Only a few people find the narrow gate."* The wide gate symbolizes life in the world. Many will choose not to serve God because they prefer to live in a way that is pleasing to them. Matthew said that the gate leading to Heaven is narrow. That is because in choosing to serve God, we also choose to give up many things that the world offers, and many people are not willing to do that. Personally, I think that the people who walk towards the narrow gate are smart. What can the world offer that is truly good for us? (Class discussion)

There is something that you need to always remember: there is only one devil, and he's nothing like God. Satan *cannot* be everywhere at once. He can't read your mind, so he doesn't know what you're thinking. He is not allowed to do anything that you won't allow. If you have the Holy Ghost inside of you, it gives you power over Satan and over sin!

The choices that you make throughout your life will determine (or decide) where you will spend eternity [*Time without an end*[38]]. Let's look at the two choices and their results.

Satan's Plan

To deceive: *To mislead the mind; to cause to err; to cause to believe what is false, or disbelieve what is true; to impose on; to delude*[39] **(John 8:44 GW)** *"...The devil was a murderer from the beginning. He has never been truthful. He doesn't know what the truth is. Whenever he tells a lie, he's doing what comes naturally to him. He's a liar and the father of lies."*

To trick: *To deceive; to impose on; to defraud; to cheat*[40] **(Ephesians 6:11)** Put on the armor of God so that you can stand against Satan's tricks!

To cause sin: (1 John 3:8a GW) *"The person who lives a sinful life belongs to the devil, because the devil has been committing sin since the beginning."*

To destroy: (1 Peter 5:8 BBE) *"Be serious and keep watch; the Evil One, who is against you, goes about like a lion with open mouth in search of food..."*

The world tries to make sin look attractive (or pretty). There are picture advertisements in magazines and on billboards. All of these things try to show people having *fun*. However, what is the real story behind the products that they are advertising? You never see pictures of the people who are in the hospital, sick with cancer caused by the cigarettes they smoked. You don't see a picture of the drunk driver who is in jail because he drove after drinking and caused a horrible accident. How much fun do you think he's having then? If you are not careful, the devil will do all he can to trap you with his tricks and vices (habits) that will cause you to become stuck in his plan.

The devil is very interested in you! Notice, I did not say that he cares for you, or loves you! He simply wants to keep you as far away from God as he possibly can. Satan knows that he is already defeated and doomed to a life in Hell, and he wants to take as many of us with him as possible. You see, Hell wasn't created for us! It was prepared for the devil and his angels. **(Matthew 25:41) (2 Peter 2:4)**

In **Hebrews 11**, the Bible talks about what happened to Moses when he faced an important, life-changing decision. **(Hebrews 11:24-26 CEV)** *"Then after Moses grew up, his faith made him refuse to be called the king's grandson. He chose to be mistreated with God's people instead of having the good time that sin could bring for a little while. Moses knew that the treasures of Egypt were not as wonderful as what he would receive from suffering for the Messiah, and he looked forward to his reward."* Moses could have continued to live in Pharaoh's house and enjoy all of the earthly pleasures that were available to him. He was a prince and most likely lived in a beautiful palace. He probably had servants, lots of money, beautiful clothes, and could have done just about anything he wanted. Instead, he traded all of those things to serve God because he knew that it held a greater reward.

God's plan

To forgive our sins: (1 John 1:9 KJV) *"If we confess our sins, he is faithful and just to forgive us our sins, and to cleanse us from all unrighteousness."*

To always love us: (John 15:12-13 KJV) *"This is my commandment, That ye love one another, as I have loved you. Greater love hath no man than this, that a man lay down his life for his friends."* Jesus loved us so much that He died for each and every one of us!

---

[38] "Eternity." *Merriam-Webster.com*. Merriam-Webster, n.d. Web. 11 Aug. 2014. <http://www.merriam-webster.com/dictionary/eternity>
[39] Noah Webster's 1828 Dictionary of American English
[40] Noah Webster's 1828 Dictionary of American English

To take care of our needs: (Matthew 6:31-34 CEV) *"Don't worry and ask yourselves, "Will we have anything to eat? Will we have anything to drink? Will we have any clothes to wear? Only people who don't know God are always worrying about such things. Your Father in heaven knows that you need all of these. But more than anything else, put God's work first and do what he wants. Then the other things will be yours as well. Don't worry about tomorrow. It will take care of itself. You have enough to worry about today."*

To take us to Heaven: (John 14:1-3 KJV) *"Let not your heart be troubled: ye believe in God, believe also in me. In my Father's house are many mansions: if it were not so, I would have told you. I go to prepare a place for you. And if I go and prepare a place for you, I will come again, and receive you unto myself; that where I am, there ye may be also."*

(Luke 4:18, 19 GW) *"The Spirit of the Lord is with me. He has anointed me to tell the Good News to the poor. He has sent me to announce forgiveness to the prisoners of sin and the restoring of sight to the blind, to forgive those who have been shattered by sin, to announce the year of the Lord's favor."*

The Bible records so many promises from God that we could not possibly fit them all into this lesson. However, we wanted to choose a few just to show you that God has great things in store for anyone who chooses to give their life completely to Him!

Now, you have heard about both God's and Satan's plans. Which one sounds better to you? Here's one more scripture that makes God's plan sound even better: **(Jeremiah 29:11 GW)** *"I know the plans that I have for you, declares the LORD. They are plans for peace and not disaster, plans to give you a future filled with hope."* God truly has nothing but good thoughts towards us. In a world where so many people say and do hurtful things to each other, isn't it wonderful that we can serve a God that loves us like Jesus does?

I want to choose God's plan and path for my life, don't you?

WHAT IS THE RAPTURE?

Lesson suggestion: *Whiteboard, markers.*

Next to receiving the Holy Ghost, the greatest event in the life of a Christian will come when Jesus comes back to gather His church together; that is when He will take us to Heaven to be with Him forever. You have most likely heard someone talk about the rapture of the church. It's often talked about in the Bible, although the actual word "rapture" isn't always used.

The word *"rapture"* means *"transport."* [41] *"Transport"* means *"to remove from one place to another."*[42] When applying the meaning to this lesson, it means that those who are serving Jesus in truth will be removed from the earth and taken to Heaven! I get so excited just thinking about it!

How do we know that Jesus will really come back?

There are promises in the Bible that tell us so! Forty days after Jesus rose from the dead, He ascended (or went up) to Heaven. **(Acts 1:3)** After He was gone, the disciples just stood there, looking up into the sky after him. **(Acts 1:10-11 BBE)** *"And while they were looking up to heaven with great attention, two men came to them, in white clothing, And said, O men of Galilee, why are you looking up into heaven? <u>This Jesus, who was taken from you into heaven, will come again, in the same way as you saw him go into heaven.</u>"* (Additional formatting by author) The angels told the disciples that Jesus would be coming back!

Another promise is located in **1 Peter 1:4-7:** *"God has something stored up for you in heaven, where it will never decay or be ruined or disappear. You have faith in God, whose power will protect you until the last day. Then he will save you, just as he has always planned to do. On that day you will be glad, even if you have to go through many hard trials for a while. Your faith will be like gold that has been tested in a fire. And these trials will prove that your faith is worth much more than gold that can be destroyed. They will show that you will be given praise and honor and glory <u>when Jesus Christ returns</u>."* **(CEV)** (Additional formatting by author)

Where will those who are raptured go?

(1 Thessalonians 4:16-17 CEV) *"With a loud command and with the shout of the chief angel and a blast of God's trumpet, <u>the Lord will return from heaven</u>. Then those who had faith in Christ before they died will be raised to life. Next, <u>all of us who are still alive will be taken up into the clouds together with them to meet the Lord in the sky</u>. From that time on we will all be with the Lord forever."* (Additional formatting by author)

What will Heaven be like?

(Matthew 13:44-46 CEV) *"The kingdom of heaven is like what happens when someone finds treasure hidden in a field and buries it again. A person like that is happy and goes and sells everything in order to buy that field. The kingdom of heaven is like what happens when a shop owner is looking for fine pearls. After finding a very valuable one, the owner goes and sells everything in order to buy that pearl."* God gave the apostle John a vision of Heaven. Imagine what it must have been like to experience that!

(Revelation 21:10, 23 KJV) *"And he carried me away in the spirit to a great and high mountain, and showed me that great city, the holy Jerusalem, descending out of heaven from God...and the city had no need of the sun, neither of the moon, to shine in it: for the glory of God did lighten it, and the Lamb is the light thereof."*

---

[41] Noah Webster's 1828 Dictionary of American English
[42] Noah Webster's 1828 Dictionary of American English

When will the rapture happen?

(Matthew 24:36-44 GW) *"No one knows when that day or hour will come. Even the angels in heaven and the Son don't know. Only the Father knows. When the Son of Man comes again, it will be exactly like the days of Noah. In the days before the flood, people were eating, drinking, and getting married until the day that Noah went into the ship. They were not aware of what was happening until the flood came and swept all of them away. That is how it will be when the Son of Man comes again. At that time two men will be working in the field. One will be taken, and the other one will be left. Two women will be working at a mill. One will be taken, and the other one will be left. Therefore, be alert, because you don't know on what day your Lord will return. You realize that if a homeowner had known at what time of the night a thief was coming, he would have stayed awake. He would not have let the thief break into his house. Therefore, you, too, must be ready because the Son of Man will return when you least expect him."*

(Mark 13:34-37 LITV) *"As a man going away, leaving his house, and giving his slaves authority, and to each his work (and he commanded the doorkeeper, that he watch), then you watch, for you do not know when the lord of the house is coming, at evening, or at midnight, or at cockcrowing, or early; so that he may not come suddenly and find you sleeping. And what I say to you, I say to all. Watch!"*

No one knows the exact day or hour when Jesus will come back for those who love Him with all of their hearts. We must live for Jesus as if we expect Him to come each moment! If we do this, the fear of being "left behind" when He comes back will never bother us. God doesn't want us to worry. He wants us to be excited about His coming! **(Luke 21:28b KJV)** *"...look up, and lift up your heads; for your redemption draweth nigh."*

Who will go in the rapture?

In order for us to go to Heaven, we must follow the plan of salvation explained in the Bible.

(Acts 2:38-39 KJV) *"Then Peter said unto them, Repent, and be baptized every one of you in the name of Jesus Christ for the remission of sins, and ye shall receive the gift of the Holy Ghost. For the promise is unto you, and to your children, and to all that are afar off, even as many as the Lord our God shall call."*

(Acts 4:12 KJV) *"Neither is there salvation in any other: for there is none other name under heaven given among men, whereby we must be saved."*

Once we have repented, been baptized in Jesus' Name, and received the Holy Ghost as evidenced by speaking in other tongues, we are "rapture-ready." However, the responsibility to Him doesn't end there. We must then choose to live a holy life, separated from sin.

- **(Leviticus 20:26 CEV)** *"I am the LORD, the holy God. You have been chosen to be my people, and so you must be holy too."*
- **(1 Peter 1:16 KJV)** *"Because it is written, Be ye holy; for I am holy."* If we do not faithfully follow God's Word, we will not go to Heaven.
- **(Matthew 7:21 GNT)** *"Not everyone who calls me 'Lord, Lord' will enter the Kingdom of heaven, but only those who do what my Father in heaven wants them to do."*
(Acts 1:4, 5; 2:4; 8:17; 10:44-48; Leviticus 20:7)

Not only are we supposed to live a holy and separated life, we are supposed to be a witness of Jesus to others. **Being** a witness of Jesus simply means that we share the good things about Him with others! **(Matthew 28:19 KJV)** *"Go ye therefore, and teach all nations, baptizing them in the name of the Father, and of the Son, and of the Holy Ghost: Teaching them to observe all things whatsoever I have commanded you..."*

We are supposed to tell others of what God has done for us. It isn't enough for us to simply live for Jesus. We must share Him!

How can I make sure I'm ready for the rapture?

God's Word is just like a big instruction book, for it holds all of the answers to salvation! Some people even call it the "Road Map for Life." As long as we follow what it says, we cannot go wrong!

- **(Matthew 6:19-21 RSV)** *"Do not lay up for yourselves treasures on earth, where moth and rust consume and where thieves break in and steal, but lay up for yourselves treasures in heaven, where neither moth nor rust consumes and where thieves do not break in and steal. For where your treasure is, there will your heart be also."*
- **(Matthew 5:3 CEV)** *"God blesses those people who depend only on him. They belong to the kingdom of heaven!"*
- **(Matthew 18:4 KJV)** *"Whosoever therefore shall humble himself as this little child, the same is greatest in the kingdom of heaven."*

We have hope!

- **(John 14:1-3 KJV)** *"Let not your heart be troubled: ye believe in God, believe also in me. In my Father's house are many mansions: if it were not so, I would have told you. I go to prepare a place for you. And if I go and prepare a place for you, I will come again, and receive you unto myself; that where I am, there ye may be also."*
- **(II Timothy 4:8 MKJV)** *"Now there is laid up for me the crown of righteousness, which the Lord, the righteous Judge, shall give me at that Day; and not to me only, but also to all those who love His appearing."*

I can't wait to see Jesus, can you? I am so excited about my heavenly Daddy coming, because He's been preparing a special place just for us!

HEAVEN OR HELL:
What's Your Destination?

Lesson suggestion: Please note: this lesson is not intended to be distressing to the students. The goal is to inform, <u>not produce fear</u>, so we should never lean towards "scary or morbid" while getting a point across. Humor and interesting facts have been mixed together! Simply illustrating the descriptions while using a white board and different colored markers, and drawing each picture while reading the verses (possibly putting an x over the "bad" things that would not be in Heaven) is very effective.

When God created man, He gave us what we call a "will," or the ability to choose how we live our life. Adam and Eve had only two rules that they had to remember **(Genesis 2:15-17)**:

1. **Rule the earth (they were "in charge" of all creation).**
2. **Don't eat of the tree in the middle of the garden, the "Tree of the Knowledge of Good and Evil."**

Adam did not know anything about evil until he and Eve ate of the "Tree of the Knowledge of Good and Evil," yet within themselves, they had the ability to choose to disobey God.

Every time we make a choice, there is either a reward or punishment that comes with it. Each choice may seem insignificant (or small), but the consequence of our choice is still there (e.g. if we choose to not go to sleep until late at night, we will be tired in the morning). In **Revelation 20:10-15**, John talks about a time that we call the "Great White Throne Judgment." This is when Jesus will sit on His throne and judge our lives. Let's look at the final reward, or punishment, that we will face: Heaven or Hell.

What is Hell?

(Teacher note: Remember to keep this part of the lesson light-hearted, as you want the children to understand that it is a very bad place, but don't want to create bad dreams.)
Hell is the home of the devil, his helpers, and those who do not choose to follow Christ. It is a place of horrible misery and suffering. The Bible describes Hell in several verses. Let's look at them to see what it will be like.

Mark 9:47-48	Jesus mentions there will be fire and worms. (Yuck! Ewww!)
Luke 16:23-24	In the story about Lazarus and the rich man, the rich man was thirsty because of the heat from the hot fire (no water was available there).
2 Peter 2:4	This verse talks of darkness or gloom. You may ask, "How can there be fire while it is dark?" Have you ever seen yellow or blue flames? Did you know that this color change is because the fire becomes hotter? Can you imagine a fire that is so hot that the color of the flame is black?
Matthew 13:49-50	This verse says that there will be darkness and wailing and gnashing of teeth. One translation adds "because of the pain." Have you ever been hurt, and it seemed that the only way to lessen the pain was to clench your teeth? That's what this verse is talking about.
Revelation 20:10-15	Again, we have fire, but added in this verse is brimstone, which is another word for sulfur. Have you ever smelled a rotten egg? Eggs have sulfur in them. When an egg rots, that sulfur gas is released. Can you imagine spending eternity in a place that smells like rotten eggs? (Yuck!)

Why did God create Hell?

That was a horrible picture of Hell! Why would God make such a bad place? Let's look at the Bible. **Read Matthew 25:41** (prepared for the devil and his angels) and **2 Peter 2:4** (punishment for angels).

"Wait," you may say! "I thought Hell was for people who were bad!" No, Hell was created for Satan and the angels that followed him in his fight against God! So, what did God build for people to go for eternity? Let's look at Heaven and see if we can find the answer.

What is Heaven?

Heaven is where God lives, where the angels live, and if we live for Jesus like we should, it is where we will live after He comes again! The Bible has a lot to say about Heaven. It is spoken about much more than hell. Let's look at just a few verses:

John 14:2	Can you imagine living in a mansion?
Hebrews 4:8-11	Doesn't it feel good to arrive home at the end of a hard day? You can be comfortable and relaxed. There will be no more hard days at school in Heaven, just rest!
2 Corinthians 12:2-4	How would you describe paradise? Anything that you can imagine will not even come close to describing what Heaven will be like!
Revelation 21:10-21	These verses give a beautiful description of Heaven. Can you imagine living in a place where the streets are made of gold? Now, this is only describing one city: the New Jerusalem. But do you know how big this city will be? The New Jerusalem will be approximately 1,400 miles cubed (New York, NY, to Tulsa, OK = 1346.2 miles). That means that it will not only be that large from north to south and from east to west, but also from top to bottom!

Heaven will be a wonderful place. **(Revelation 22:5)** There will be no more night, no crying, and no sadness; none of the bad things that we experience on earth will be there. Don't you want to go?

Why did God create Heaven?

We looked at why God made Hell. Now, let's look at why He created Heaven:

John 14:2-4	Jesus said, *"I go to prepare a place for you."* Heaven is for *us*!
Revelation 22:14	Only we who have "washed our robes," or have lived according to His Word, can enter into this city.
Matthew 7:21	Only those who obey His voice can enter.

Did you notice that God didn't even want to consider the possibility of one person not wanting to live for Him? God wants so much for everyone to spend eternity with Him that He did not even prepare a place of punishment for people who refused Him! Hell was made for the angels that rebelled in Heaven. If we refuse Jesus' salvation, He has no choice but to place us in Hell because there is no place of punishment made for man.

God has made a city of mansions for us to live, a place so beautiful that the streets are paved with gold! Don't you want to spend eternity with Him? How about taking your friends with you?

WHAT IS LOVE?

Lesson suggestion: Whiteboard, markers.

Love is a word that is overused today. We say that we "love" chocolate candy, certain movies, skating, and playing video games. But, do we really know what love is? Let's look at love from God's eyes.

(John 3:16) Jesus died for you. Would you die for chocolate candy? (I like to eat it, but I certainly wouldn't die for it!) God expects us to love Him! **(Deuteronomy 6:4-5 KJV)** *"Hear, O Israel: the Lord our God is one Lord: And thou shalt love the Lord thy God with all thine heart, and with all thy soul, and with all thy might."* **(Genesis 22:2-18)** God tested Abraham's love for Him by asking him to sacrifice Isaac. **Just what is love?**

<u>1 Corinthians 13: 1-13 CEV</u>:

Verse 1: *"What if I could speak all languages of humans and of angels? If I did not love others, I would be nothing more than a noisy gong or a clanging cymbal."*

- Just think of what you could do if you could speak many languages! You could be a missionary to any country in the world. Or, if you knew the language of the angels, you could direct them to do many good things, or ask them questions. But without love, it would just be noise.

Verse 2: *"What if I could prophesy and understand all secrets and all knowledge? And what if I had faith that moved mountains? I would be nothing, unless I loved others."*

- What would it be like if you knew the future, knew all secrets, and had all faith? Just think of what you could accomplish! You could stop bad things from happening, have your prayers answered immediately... The list of what you could do would be endless! But think about this: even if you could do all of those things, it would be of no value if you didn't have love.

Verse 3: *"What if I gave away all that I owned and let myself be burned alive? I would gain nothing, unless I loved others."*

- Surely if I gave everything I owned, or sacrificed my life, people would think I was great! But God says that without love, my efforts would be useless.

Verse 4: *"Love is kind and patient, never jealous, boastful, proud, or..."*

- Is kind. **(Ephesians 4:32 KJV)** *"And be ye kind one to another..."*

- Patient (patience is also a fruit of the Spirit). *(1 Thessalonians 5:14 KJV)* *"...be patient toward all men."*

- Jealous. **(James 3:13-14 GW)** *"Do any of you have wisdom and insight? Show this by living the right way with the humility that comes from wisdom. But if you are bitterly jealous and filled with self-centered ambition, don't brag. Don't say that you are wise when it isn't true."*

- Boastful. Bragging; haughty. **(Psalms 12:3-4 GNB)** *"Silence those flattering tongues, O LORD! Close those boastful mouths that say, "With our words we get what we want. We will say what we wish, and no one can stop us.""*

- Proud. **(Proverbs 21:24 GNB)** *"Show me a conceited person and I will show you someone who is arrogant, proud, and inconsiderate."*

Verse 5: *"...rude. Love isn't selfish or quick tempered. It doesn't keep a record of wrongs that others do."*

- Rude. Indecent, unbecoming, rude, impolite. Did you realize your manners show if you love something or someone?
- Selfish. **(Proverbs 28:25 GW)** *"A greedy person stirs up a fight, but whoever trusts the LORD prospers."*
- Quick-tempered. **(Proverbs 12:16 NLT)** *"A fool is quick-tempered, but a wise person stays calm when insulted."*
- Doesn't keep a record *(doesn't remember)*. **(Isaiah 43:18 GW)** *"Forget what happened in the past, and do not dwell on events from long ago."*

Verse 6: *"Love rejoices in the truth, but not in evil."*

- Rejoices in the truth. Honesty, integrity, sincerity. **(Proverbs 23:23 CEV)** *"Invest in truth and wisdom, discipline and good sense, and don't part with them."*

Verse 7: *"Love is always supportive, loyal, hopeful, and trusting."*

- Supportive. Quiet patience; not complaining. **(Psalms 139:9-10 NLT)** *"If I ride the wings of the morning, if I dwell by the farthest oceans, even there Your hand will guide me, and Your strength will support me."*
- Loyal. Trusts; does not question. This verse explains loyalty: **(2 Samuel 3:1 NLT)** *"That was the beginning of a long war between those who were loyal to Saul and those loyal to David. As time passed David became stronger and stronger, while Saul's dynasty became weaker and weaker."*
- Hopeful. Faith. **(Hebrews 11:1 KJV)** *"Now faith is the substance of things hoped for..."*
- Trusting. **(Hebrews 3:14 NLT)** *"For if we are faithful to the end, trusting God just as firmly as when we first believed, we will share in all that belongs to Christ."*

Verse 8: *"Love never fails! Everyone who prophesies will stop, and unknown languages will no longer be spoken. All that we know will be forgotten."*

- Never fails. In the KJV, the word used for "faileth" means more than outright failure, but means inefficient as well. *Inefficient*: Wasteful of time, energy, or materials. [43] Unproductive, wasteful, ineffective, and disorganized.

Verses 9-12: *"We don't know everything, and our prophecies are not complete. But what is perfect will someday appear, and what isn't perfect will then disappear. When we were children, we thought and reasoned as children do. But when we grew up, we quit our childish ways. Now all we can see of God is like a cloudy picture in a mirror. Later we will see him face to face. We don't know everything, but then we will, just as God completely understands us."*

- As we mature in our walk with God, we will be better able to understand love. We will be spending time with "love." **(1 John 4:8 KJV)** *"God is love."*

Verse 13: *"For now there are faith, hope, and love. But of these three, the greatest is love."*

- Faith. Persuasion, moral conviction – Faith in God for salvation.
- Hope. Expectation, confidence – Our hope is in the power of Jesus.
- Love. Pure love – Love that comes from God. **(1 John 4:7-21)**

---

[43] Webster's II New Riverside Dictionary, pg. 625.

God wants us to realize just how important "love" is to Him. If we do not, or cannot, love ourselves or others, then we are not truly His children.

We all know that "hate" is the opposite of love, but have you thought about "indifference?" (That is another word for the phrase "I don't care.") Indifference is worse than hate, because at least hate will cause you to react. If you love sinners, you will try to help them. If you hate sin, you will try to help those that are trapped by it. *If you are indifferent, you will do nothing.*

Jesus wants us to have love in our life, for this is the only way that He can show love to those who do not know Him. We may be the only "Jesus" that someone will ever see or meet.

"...The most important commandment is this: 'Listen, O Israel! The LORD our God is the one and only LORD. And you must love the LORD your God with all your heart, all your soul, all your mind, and all your strength.' The second is equally important: 'Love your neighbor as yourself.' No other commandment is greater than these." **(Mark 12:29-31 NLT)**

SINCE GOD IS LOVE, IS THERE ANYTHING HE HATES?

Lesson suggestion: Whiteboard, markers.

We have learned that "God is love." But, while He loves us unconditionally, we still do not have the right to sin. God loved us so much that He came and died on a cross so that we would be able to overcome sin in our lives. In this lesson, we are going to look at some of the things God hates and learn why He hates them.

(Proverbs 6:16-19 NKJV) *"These six things the Lord hates, Yes, seven are an abomination to Him: a proud look, A lying tongue, Hands that shed innocent blood, a heart that devises wicked plans, Feet that are swift in running to evil, a false witness who speaks lies, and one who sows discord among brethren."*

Let's look at each of these things to see why God has chosen to hate them.

A proud look, or haughty eyes

Why does God hate pride? Could it be that pride causes one to think of himself as better than others? Can you really be unified with other people if you have pride? A true team doesn't have star players. Rather, it has players who are unified, helping each other, and working together to win a game. The Apostle Paul, who is considered by many to be the greatest evangelist in the New Testament, said that he was chief (or the worst) among sinners, not saints. *"In the same way, you younger men must accept the authority of the elders. And all of you, serve each other in humility, for "God opposes the proud but favors the humble." So humble yourselves under the mighty power of God, and at the right time He will lift you up in honor. Give all your worries and cares to God, for He cares about you."* **(1 Peter 5:5-7 NLT)** [Humility: the quality or state of not thinking you are better than other people: the quality or state of being humble.[44]] [Humble: not proud or haughty: not arrogant or assertive[45]]

A lying tongue

Notice that Proverbs 6:17 does not say "lies," but a lying tongue. Yes, it is a sin to lie, but this goes deeper. Have you ever known someone who had a reputation for lying? If they said, "The sun is shining," you would run and get an umbrella because you could not trust what they told you. This is what God is talking about in this verse. Why? How can you believe someone you cannot trust? How easy would it be to work with someone, to reach those who do not know Jesus, if you cannot trust what they is saying? If a person habitually lies, who is their "father?" *"Your father is the devil, and you do exactly what he wants. He has always been a murderer and a liar. There is nothing truthful about him. He speaks on his own, and everything he says is a lie. Not only is he a liar himself, but he is also the father of all lies."* **(John 8:44 CEV)**

Hands that kill the innocent

This one is easy to understand; however, this is talking about more than just killing someone. **Read Proverbs 18:21 and James 3:8.** Have you ever shed "innocent blood" with words that you said? How do you reach your friends at school if they are afraid to confide in you? Can they trust you if they know that you gossip and talk about them to other people? *"You shall not kill."* **(Exodus 20:13 MKJV)**

---

[44] *Merriam-Webster.com*. Merriam-Webster, n.d. Web. 7 Oct. 2014. <http://www.merriam-webster.com/dictionary/humility>.
[45] *Merriam-Webster.com*. Merriam-Webster, n.d. Web. 7 Oct. 2014. <http://www.merriam-webster.com/dictionary/humble>.

A heart that plots evil

We all enjoy having fun, and we even enjoy teasing each other sometimes. However, do we ever cross a line where teasing becomes "evil," when we are actually hurting the other person with our words? God hates this. How can you hurt your brother one moment and lift him up the next? *"Do not plan ways of harming one another. Do not give false testimony under oath. I hate lying, injustice, and violence."* **(Zechariah 8:17 GNB)**

Feet that race to do wrong

To cause "mischief" is to play pranks, to embarrass someone intentionally, or to annoy someone. If you are known for your pranks (teasing and tricks on others), people will not trust you. Are you always looking for some kind of mischief to get into? How can you witness to someone about Jesus if they don't trust you? Will they believe what you say? *"They rush to commit evil deeds. They hurry to commit murder. If a bird sees a trap being set, it knows to stay away."* **(Proverbs 1:16-17 NLT)**

A false witness who pours out lies

This was one of the Ten Commandments given to Moses. Have you ever known someone who liked to tell stories? We also call those types of stories "fibs." [Fib: an untrue statement about something minor or unimportant: a trivial or childish lie.[46]] The story gets bigger each time they tell it, and this creates a problem. How do you know when they are telling the truth? Would you believe them if they told you that God caused a blind person to see? How can you work in God's kingdom with someone you do not trust? *"Do not tell lies about others."* **(Exodus 20:16 CEV)**

He who sows discord among brothers

Discord is another word for strife. When someone creates strife, they are making a situation occur where people argue with each other. [Strife: very angry or violent disagreement between two or more people or groups.[47]] People who struggle with strife simply just can't, or refuse to, get along with other people! This is also called contention, and can also refer to someone who tries to establish his or her own group of friends, or clique. *"They are always thinking up something cruel and evil, and they stir up trouble."* **(Proverbs 6:14 CEV)**

God's special dream is that all of His people would work together as members of one big family. However, if we allow ourselves to be caught up in any of the things that we've learned about today, they will keep us from working together. Rather than working against each other, we should be working with each other, for that is what Jesus would do!

---

[46] *Merriam-Webster.com*. Merriam-Webster, n.d. Web. 4 Aug. 2014. <http://www.merriam-webster.com/dictionary/fib>.
[47] *Merriam-Webster.com*. Merriam-Webster, n.d. Web. 4 Aug. 2014. <http://www.merriam-webster.com/dictionary/strife>.

YOU WANT ME TO FAST? BUT, I'M JUST A KID!

Lesson suggestion: *Fasting Commitment Card (located in the Teacher's Toolbox), table, bottle of water, bottle of juice, can of soup, candy bar, part of a fresh vegetable, a piece of fresh fruit, "pleasure reading" book, video, computer game, slice of bread, can of pop (preferably one with a lot of caffeine, like Mt. Dew), and mustard seed. Also, consider having homemade cookies for everyone to enjoy at the close of the lesson! (Wait until you are nearing the lesson's conclusion before you begin letting the children view your "examples.")*

Oh, boy, here we go! We've heard a lot about fasting, but why are we supposed to do it? All we know is that when our parents fast, they get hungry, and that does *not* sound like fun! How can fasting benefit us? It can't be good for our bodies to go without food, right?

This is the attitude that many people take when it comes to fasting! We love to talk about things we like to eat, but we have a *really* hard time even *thinking* about going *without* them!

Why should we fast? Why is it necessary?

To grow closer to God; for a deeper relationship with Him; to know Him better.
Read Acts 10:30-31. Cornelius wanted to know God better. God noticed Cornelius' fasting and prayers, and how serious he was about his relationship with God. Because of this, God sent Peter to Cornelius and his family, which resulted in all of them receiving the Holy Ghost!

To operate with gifts in the Spirit
Read Matthew 17:14-21. The disciples did not understand that they could not heal the boy's illness because they didn't have true faith; they didn't believe that their prayers would actually work! From this scripture, you can see that we only need to have faith as small as a grain of mustard seed in order to see miracles happen!

To overcome sin in our life
Read Jonah 3:5. The people of Nineveh were great sinners. They saw their need for God, and then fasted in order to cleanse themselves from sin. As a result, God saw their repentance and spared their city from destruction.

How can we overcome our flesh on a daily (or everyday) basis? By praying and reading our Bibles! Fasting is another great way to keep ourselves right before God. When you don't feed your body food, it begins sending different signals to your brain (by growling, gurgling) because it is trying to tell you, "Eat! I am *hungry*!" However, when you fast, *you become the boss of your body* (or flesh)! It's called putting your "flesh under submission." You're telling your body what to do, which is to focus on your relationship with God. He honors that. *(Teacher: if you have a testimony resulting from a fast, this would be a good time to share it with your students.)*

Submission is a big word! Has anyone learned about root words in school? What do you think the root word of submission would be? (Submit) Submit is a word that means *"to yield, resign or surrender to the power, will or authority of another"*[48]. In other words, it means to obey! So *submission* means *"obedience; compliance with the commands or laws of a superior."*[49] Wow! You didn't know that you had so much power, did you? When you fast, you make laws that your body has to obey! Isn't that *cool*? You are young, and it's very likely that going without more than one meal would be very difficult for you, since your bodies are constantly growing. However, did you know that you could choose to fast different sorts of things, such as candy? Or videos and television? Or computer games?

---

[48] Noah Webster's 1828 Dictionary of American English
[49] Noah Webster's 1828 Dictionary of American English

(Let the viewing of your items begin! As you introduce each one, inquire about their favorite foods, snacks, candy, videos, etc. You'll be amazed at what you will learn about your students! You can also talk about priorities: what is really important to us, what really matters and what doesn't, etc. Take advantage of the opportunity to be a thought-provoker!)

When we choose to do without something that we really like, we are telling our flesh *"No!"* That may sound funny to you, but it is necessary! When our flesh does not "obey" us, it is easier for the devil to convince us to do things that we should not do.

Pass out a Fasting Commitment Card set to each student.

Now that we have learned about the importance of fasting, and how it strengthens our relationship with God, I want you to ask you a question. Are you willing to take part in a week of fasting with me? I would like to help you learn how to create this habit in your life. Let's take a minute to pray together and ask Jesus how we can begin. While you're praying, ask Him what sacrifice He would like you to make. Listen very carefully. Afterwards, we will write it down on the card that I gave to you.

Next week, we will share testimonies of good things that happen to us during our week of fasting. I am already looking forward to the victory reports that I will hear from each of you, because I know that God always honors sacrifice!

Author's note: *The top copy of the Fasting Commitment Card is theirs to take home, and the bottom one is for you to keep; we suggest even giving a copy of the cards to your pastor.*

We suggest a weeklong period. Make sure the kids do not set a goal that exceeds their ability (e.g. fasting 3 days). They must understand that starting slow and building is the way to endurance! Make sure that the parents/guardians know of their child's commitment, as encouragement from them will help the children succeed in achieving their goal.

WHY DO WE GIVE TITHES AND OFFERINGS?

Lesson suggestion: *Whiteboard, markers. If you are teaching in a church setting, consider having a tithing envelope available so that at some point in the lesson, you can explain the procedure that your church follows.*

Have you ever noticed that an offering is taken during every service that you attend? Have you ever wondered why? Today, we are going to look in the Bible and see if there is a reason for this happening so often.

Is it important to give an offering to God?

Did you know that 504 verses in the Bible use the word "offering" (KJV), while there are just 216 verses that use the word "praise" (KJV)? Yet, in **Psalms 22:3**, the Bible says that He inhabits (or sits in) our praises. This must mean that giving is *very* important to have been mentioned so many more times!

Adam and his sons gave the first offerings that we read about in the Bible. In fact, nearly every important person in the Old Testament gave an offering. In those days, cattle and sheep were the same as money.

In early history, many farmers paid their bills using what we call the "barter system." This means that they would trade whatever they had for the supplies that they needed. For example, if they needed to buy a plow, they might bring a cow into the blacksmith to trade for it. Today, we use money to both buy the things that we want and to give offerings to God.

The giving of an offering is always associated with worship. Read **1 Chronicles 16:27-30 and Psalms 96:6-9.** People generally give money for the things that interest them the most. Let's look at ourselves. What do we do that brings us the most pleasure? A girl may enjoy playing with dolls, and a boy may enjoy sports. Maybe you enjoy video games! Is it easy to spend money on these things? (Of course) We all know that it is, because stores set aside an entire section just for these types of things! Can you imagine *(name a store that is popular in your area)* without a toy department?

We should look at God in the same way. He died for our sins and then arose from the grave; then, He went to Heaven and is there preparing a special place for us to live during eternity. Is there anything you want more than to go to Heaven?

Think about this: What if everyone that went to McDonald's stopped paying for the food that they ate? It wouldn't be long before the company would no longer have money to make food, would it? We don't want this to happen to our church, do we?

God chose to provide for the needs of his ministers (preachers) through people like you and me. We do this by giving our tithes and offerings. "Tithes" is a word that is not used much today. In fact, you probably would not hear it at all if you did not attend church! *"Tithe"* simply means *"a tenth."* For example, ten dimes are equal to one dollar, so a tithe (or a tenth) of one dollar is one dime.

Genesis 14:18-20 tells us that Abraham gave the first tithe in the Bible. We hear about tithing again when God gave Moses instructions about the Tabernacle *(discussed in the book of Leviticus; see 27:30).* In His instructions, God gave a command that every family had to bring a tithe to the Tabernacle. The tithes were given in order to supply the needs of the priest, who received their food from a portion of the sacrifices that were offered. However, just as the priests received a portion of the other peoples' tithe offering (sacrifice) for food, *they* also had to bring their tithes as well. *No one* was exempt (excluded, or not included) in the command of tithing.

Just as the Israelites' tithe supplied the needs of the Tabernacle and priests, our tithes supply the needs of the church and ministry. This is why *everyone's* tithe is important. You may be asking yourself, "What does this have to do with me? I don't own a house, cattle, or much of anything else! I'm just a kid!"

Let's look at **Deuteronomy 14:22**: *"Thou shalt truly tithe all the increase of thy seed, that the field bringeth forth year by year."* **(KJV)** In **2 Chronicles 31:4-6** it says, *"He told the people of Jerusalem to bring the offerings that were to be given to the priests and Levites, so that they would have time to serve the LORD with their work. As soon as the people heard what the king wanted, they brought a tenth of everything they owned, including their best grain, wine, olive oil, honey, and other crops. The people from the other towns of Judah brought a tenth of their herds and flocks, as well as a tenth of anything they had dedicated to the LORD."* **(CEV)** We pay our tithes on our "increase," which refers to our income (money that we have earned). How do you receive an increase? Do you get paid to do chores, or do you receive an allowance? Have you ever received birthday or Christmas money? There are many different ways that you could receive an increase!

Maybe you think that since you don't have much money, your tithe wouldn't go very far because it's so small. What would God do with your little bit? That's a great question, and the answer is found in the Bible! Let's read **Mark 12:41-44**: *"Jesus was sitting in the temple near the offering box and watching people put in their gifts. He noticed that many rich people were giving a lot of money. Finally, a poor widow came up and put in two coins that were worth only a few pennies. Jesus told his disciples to gather around him. Then he said: I tell you that this poor widow has put in more than all the others. Everyone else gave what they didn't need. But she is very poor and gave everything she had. Now she doesn't have a cent to live on."* **(CEV)** Jesus said that because she gave all that she owned to the work of God, the widow's few pennies were worth more to Him than the offerings given by the rich.

If you still don't think that tithing is important, look at **Malachi 3:8-10**. It says, *"Can a person cheat God? Yet, you are cheating me! But you ask, How are we cheating you? When you don't bring a tenth of your income and other contributions. So a curse is on you because the whole nation is cheating me! Bring one-tenth of your income into the storehouse so that there may be food in my house. Test me in this way, says the LORD of Armies. See if I won't open the windows of heaven for you and flood you with blessings."* **(GW)** The word *cheat* can also be replaced with *rob*. The sad thing is that the Bible also says that if we rob (or cheat) God, a curse will come upon us. It is kind of like having holes in our pockets. When we do not pay our tithes, it seems like we never have enough money! On the other hand, when we pay our tithes, God will flood us with blessings. Have you ever seen a flood? *A flood happens when a river cannot hold all of its water and ends up overflowing its banks.* If God floods us with blessings, it means that we won't be able to hold all of them!

Giving to God is very important. In **2 Corinthians 9:6-12**, Paul says: *"Remember that the person who plants few seeds will have a small crop; the one who plants many seeds will have a large crop. You should each give, then, as you have decided, not with regret or out of a sense of duty; for God loves the one who gives gladly. And God is able to give you more than you need, so that you will always have all you need for yourselves and more than enough for every good cause. As the scripture says, He gives generously to the needy; his kindness lasts forever. And God, who supplies seed for the sower and bread to eat, will also supply you with all the seed you need and will make it grow and produce a rich harvest from your generosity. He will always make you rich enough to be generous at all times, so that many will thank God for your gifts which they receive from us. For this service you perform not only meets the needs of God's people, but also produces an outpouring of gratitude to God."* **(GNT)**

God wants us to give *cheerfully*. When we give to Him, God will give back to us, which enables us to give even more! As long as we are faithful to Him, He will always supply our needs. **(Philippians 4:19a KJV)** *"But my God shall supply all your need according to his riches in glory...."*

FAITH – SOMETHING THAT WE CANNOT SEE

Lesson suggestion: *Whiteboard, markers.*

You have probably heard Pastor say, "We just have to have faith!" What exactly does he mean? What does it mean to have faith? The dictionary says this: **Faith:** n. *"to persuade, to draw towards any thing, to conciliate; to believe, to obey."*[50]

There are different types of faith. In this lesson, we are going to talk about the type of faith that helps us get through our problems!

The Centurion

He believed that all Jesus had to do was say that his servant would be healed, and it would happen. Because we want instant and obvious results, that might not have been good enough for us!

(Matthew 8:5-10 NLT) *"When Jesus arrived in Capernaum, a Roman officer came and pleaded with him, "Lord, my young servant lies in bed, paralyzed and racked with pain." Jesus said, "I will come and heal him." Then the officer said, "Lord, I am not worthy to have you come into my home. Just say the word from where you are, and my servant will be healed! I know, because I am under the authority of my superior officers and I have authority over my soldiers. I only need to say, 'Go,' and they go, or 'Come,' and they come. And if I say to my slaves, 'Do this or that,' they do it." When Jesus heard this, he was amazed. Turning to the crowd, he said, "I tell you the truth, I haven't seen faith like this in all the land of Israel!"*

(2 Corinthians 5:7 KJV) *"For we walk by faith, and not by sight."*

Abraham, concerning God's request for his only son

Abraham prepared to offer Isaac to God, always believing that the Lord would provide another sacrifice.

(Genesis 22:1-19 NLT) *"Later on God tested Abraham's faith and obedience. "Abraham!" God called. "Yes," he replied. "Here I am." "Take your son, your only son—yes, Isaac, whom you love so much—and go to the land of Moriah. Sacrifice him there as a burnt offering on one of the mountains, which I will point out to you." The next morning Abraham got up early. He saddled his donkey and took two of his servants with him, along with his son Isaac. Then he chopped wood to build a fire for a burnt offering and set out for the place where God had told him to go. On the third day of the journey, Abraham saw the place in the distance. "Stay here with the donkey," Abraham told the young men. "The boy and I will travel a little farther. We will worship there, and then we will come right back." Abraham placed the wood for the burnt offering on Isaac's shoulders, while he himself carried the knife and the fire. As the two of them went on together, Isaac said, "Father?" "Yes, my son," Abraham replied. "We have the wood and the fire," said the boy, "but where is the lamb for the sacrifice?" "God will provide a lamb, my son," Abraham answered. And they both went on together. When they arrived at the place where God had told Abraham to go, he built an altar and placed the wood on it. Then he tied Isaac up and laid him on the altar over the wood. And Abraham took the knife and lifted it up to kill his son as a sacrifice to the LORD. At that moment the angel of the LORD shouted to him from heaven, "Abraham! Abraham!" "Yes," he answered. "I'm listening." "Lay down the knife," the angel said. "Do not hurt the boy in any way, for now I know that you truly fear God. You have not withheld even your beloved son from me." Then Abraham looked up and saw a ram caught by its horns in a bush. So he took the ram and sacrificed it as a burnt offering on the altar in place of his son. Abraham named the place "The LORD Will Provide." This name has now become a proverb: "On the mountain of the LORD it will be provided." Then the angel of the LORD called again to Abraham from heaven, "This is what the LORD says: Because you have obeyed me and have not withheld even your*

---

[50] Noah Webster's 1828 Dictionary of American English

beloved son, I swear by my own self that I will bless you richly. I will multiply your descendants into countless millions, like the stars of the sky and the sand on the seashore. They will conquer their enemies, and through your descendants, all the nations of the earth will be blessed—all because you have obeyed me." Then they returned to Abraham's young men and traveled home again to Beersheba, where Abraham lived for quite some time."

Many times, we cannot see what God is doing. We may need a healing, and it doesn't seem like it is coming very quickly! Maybe we have been praying every day about a problem in our family, and it just doesn't seem to be getting any better. We must remember that God's time is not the same as ours. He doesn't wear a watch and count the minutes as they go by, like we do sometimes! Can you imagine if God had a cell phone? Now, think about this. There are over 6 billion people on the planet Earth, and most of us have a problem that is important (to us) <u>at least</u> once a week!

How many of your parents have voicemail on their cell phones? (Class discussion) How many of you have seen your parents choose to not answer a phone call because they are too busy to talk right then? If we could call God, can you imagine how many different voicemails He would need? I can just imagine His voicemail message: **(Imitate a voicemail recording)** *"Hello, this is God. I am very busy right now trying to answer your prayer. If you could just have a little patience, your answer will arrive very soon. Now, please try to have a nice day."* How many of us would hang up and call right back, just to see if He was really there and just screening His calls?

We should not act like that! **Galatians 5:22, 23** says, *"But when the Holy Spirit controls our lives, he will produce this kind of fruit in us: love, joy, peace, patience, kindness, goodness, faithfulness, gentleness, and self-control."* **(NLT)**

Galatians 5:3-4 says, *"And not only so, but we glory in tribulations also: knowing that tribulation worketh patience; and patience, experience; and experience, hope:"* *(KJV)* In another translation, it says, *"We can rejoice, too, when we run into problems and trials, for we know that they are good for us—they help us learn to endure."* **(NLT)**

We need to trust God to work everything out for our good. Remember, He placed His spirit inside us as a comforter. Although things may seem rough sometimes, He really *is* in control of everything that goes on around us, and will be a friend in the middle of our problems. We simply need to pray and ask Jesus for help!

WILL GOD HEAL US?

Lesson suggestion: *Whiteboard, markers, and mustard seeds (enough for everyone in the class). Special keepsake idea: purchase a small bottle for each student, fill with olive oil and place a mustard seed inside.*

We know God can heal us, but do we believe He will?

How many times have we prayed for someone who is sick and not really expected him or her to be healed? Maybe we said, "If it is God's will, they will be healed." Then when they stay sick, we think, "Well, I guess it wasn't God's will." Was it really not God's will, or did we just not exercise our faith?

How much faith do you need?

In **Luke 17:5-6**, the disciples asked Jesus to increase their faith (make it bigger). He answered, *"If you had faith no bigger than a tiny mustard seed, you could tell this mulberry tree to pull itself up, roots and all, and to plant itself in the ocean. And it would!"* **(CEV)**

Have you ever seen a mustard seed? *(Pass out seeds)* It is very small, but if planted and watered, that small seed will grow to be 10 feet or taller! The question is not "How big is your faith?" but rather, "Has your faith been planted and watered?" In **Matthew 17:20**, Jesus said that we could move a mountain with faith the size of a mustard seed. This does not mean that we can go to Mt. Everest, speak to it and tell it to move! The mountain simply symbolizes (or stands for) something that seems very big to us (illness, dad out of a job, etc.).

Who will God heal?

The Bible mentions at least four different times when Jesus healed all that came to Him **(Matthew 4:24; 12:15: 15:30; Luke 6:19)** The Bible even mentions a time when Jesus left His plan (of only ministering to Jews) and helped a Samaritan woman because she had great faith!

The purpose of Jesus coming to earth was to save the Jews, God's chosen people. He had a specific plan: to reach the Jews, who would then be His witnesses and tell the rest of the world about Him (be witnesses). While in the midst of His miracles, He was approached by a Gentile woman who sought healing for her daughter. Because of her great faith, He changed His plan! This shows how far God will go to honor the true faith of someone who believes in Him. We read about her in **Matthew 15:21-29**: *"Jesus left and went to the territory near the cities of Tyre and Sidon. Suddenly a Canaanite woman from there came out shouting, "Lord and Son of David, have pity on me! My daughter is full of demons." Jesus did not say a word. But the woman kept following along and shouting, so his disciples came up and asked him to send her away. Jesus said, "I was sent only to the people of Israel! They are like a flock of lost sheep." The woman came closer. Then she knelt down and begged, "Please help me, Lord!" Jesus replied, "It isn't right to take food away from children and feed it to dogs." "Lord, that's true," the woman said, "but even dogs get the crumbs that fall from their owner's table." Jesus answered, "Dear woman, you really do have a lot of faith, and you will be given what you want." At that moment her daughter was healed."* **(CEV)**

Jesus used her to teach a lesson in faith. **Matthew 15:30** says, *"Large crowds came and brought many people who were crippled or blind or lame or unable to talk. They placed them, and many others, in front of Jesus, and he healed them all."* **(CEV)**

Why doesn't God heal everyone today?

Sadly, the only place He could not do many miracles was His hometown. **Read Mark 6:1-6**. Everyone in Nazareth remembered Him as a carpenter, the Son of Mary. Some of the women had probably changed his diapers when He was a baby. In **verses 5-6**, it says *"And because of their unbelief, he couldn't do any mighty miracles among them except to place his hands on a few sick people and heal them. And he was amazed at their unbelief."* **(CEV)**

You may say, "That was then. Jesus is not standing beside me now." You are right; Jesus is not physically standing beside you. However, if you have the Holy Ghost, you have something just as good, because He is living in your heart! Let's look at what can happen if you exercise your Holy Ghost power along with your faith. **(Acts 5:12-16)** After the resurrection and ascension of Jesus, the Holy Ghost had been poured out on His disciples and others who had followed Jesus. The disciples began ministering to others just as Jesus had done! Peter had become so full of the Holy Ghost that people would bring their sick friends and family members and lay them in the street, hoping that his shadow would cover them as he walked by. They were healed because of their faith!

We should always have faith that God *can*, and *will*, heal everyone! It is possible that He is waiting on us to change our actions, which will then bring healing to our body (e.g., stomach is hurting from too many sweets; if we stop eating them, the tummy ache goes away). It is also important to understand that we will not always know why God allows bad things to happen (e.g., someone close to us dies). In those instances, our faith has to enable us (or help us) to believe that God knows what is best, and that He will be with us during the hard times.

In **2 Corinthians 12:7-9**, we read that the Apostle Paul had "a thorn in the flesh" (the Bible does not tell what it was). Paul asked God to deliver him three different times, but God's answer was simply *"My grace is sufficient for you."* **(1 Corinthians 12:9 KJV)** Paul had received many revelations from God. Sometimes, when we do things that people notice and like, it is easy to feel "important." It is possible that God allowed Paul to live with this "thorn" because he was in danger of becoming prideful.

Sometimes, we think God did not answer our prayer because the person was not healed. However, maybe God's answer was just different than what we thought would, or should, happen. You see, God may not always heal us, but there is one thing you can be sure of: He will always answer our prayers! We just need to listen, like Paul, so that we hear His answer.

Now, I will ask you again. **I know you believe that Jesus can heal, but do you believe that He *will* heal when you pray?** Let's look at the difference:

(Luke 18:35-43 LITV) *"And it happened as He drew near to Jericho, a certain blind one sat by the highway, begging. And a crowd passing through, he asked what this might be. And they reported to him that Jesus the Nazarene is passing by. And he cried out, saying, Jesus, Son of David, pity me! And those going before rebuked him, that he be quiet. But he much more cried out, Son of David, pity me! And standing still, Jesus commanded him to be brought to Him. And he drawing near, He asked him, saying, What do you desire I do to you? And he said, Lord, that I may see again. And Jesus said to him, See again! Your faith has healed you. And instantly he saw again. And he followed Him, glorifying God. And seeing, all the people gave praise to God."*

(Matthew 8:2-3 BBE) *"And a leper came and gave him worship, saying, Lord, if it is your pleasure, you have power to make me clean. And he put his hand on him, saying, It is my pleasure; be clean. And straight away he was made clean."*

It is God's pleasure to heal us. He wants to! We must simply change from believing that He *can* to believing that *He will do it*!

HOW MUCH FAITH DO WE NEED?

Lesson suggestion: *Whiteboard, markers, mustard seed, a lamp and a light bulb. Make sure you have a power outlet available so that you can plug in the lamp during the lesson (the light bulb should be screwed into the lamp prior to the start of your lesson).*

I have three questions to ask, and I want you to think carefully about your answers.

1. How many of you like to pray for people?
2. Do you have faith when you pray?
3. How much faith does it take to get an answer?

In **Matthew 10:1**, Jesus gave the disciples the power to perform miracles. As we read **Matthew chapter 17**, we see that a man brought his son to the disciples to be delivered. **(Matthew 17:14-16 BBE)** *"And when they came to the people, a man went down on his knees to him, saying, Lord have mercy on my son: for he is off his head, and is in great pain; and frequently he goes falling into the fire, and frequently into the water. And I took him to your disciples, and they were not able to make him well."*

Although they prayed for him, he was <u>not</u> delivered! Why could they not deliver him? *(Ask for group response, and then read the following.)*

(Matthew 17:17-20 BBE) *"And Jesus, answering, said, O false and foolish generation, how long will I be with you? how long will I put up with you? let him come here to me. And Jesus gave orders to the unclean spirit, and it went out of him: and the boy was made well from that hour. Then the disciples came to Jesus privately, and said, Why were we not able to send it out? And he says to them, Because of your little faith: for truly I say to you, If you have faith as a grain of mustard seed, you will say to this mountain, Be moved from this place to that; and it will be moved; and nothing will be impossible to you."*

Why were they unable to heal his child? Because of their "little" faith!

But wait! Didn't Jesus also say that you only need faith the size of a mustard seed? What is so special about a mustard seed? It is the smallest seed that God created! *(Show the children a mustard seed)* In the time of Jesus, it was common for someone to refer to a mustard seed when they were talking about something tiny. He was trying to get the disciples to realize that we only have a very small part in a miracle. All we need is *tiny faith*.

So, why didn't they even have *tiny* faith? The disciples had just seen Jesus, Moses, and Elijah talking to each other **(Matthew 17:1-8)**, watched Jesus feed two large crowds of people **(Matthew 14:14-20) (Matthew 15:30-38)**, and seen Him give Peter the keys to the kingdom **(Matthew 16:13-19)**! Not only that, they had watched Jesus perform miracle…after miracle…after miracle. Wouldn't it seem easy to even have tiny faith after seeing all of these wonderful things happen?

Let's look at another example of great faith. In **Matthew 8:5-13**, the Centurion came to Jesus and asked for one of his servants to be healed (*a centurion was an officer in the Roman army who had charge over 100 men*). Jesus, always respectful of those in authority, said that He would come. However, the Centurion did something unique (very special). He stopped Jesus from coming! He said, "Jesus, I understand what it is like to be under authority. If You will only *speak the word* I know my servant will be healed." Wow! Someone who wasn't a Jew understood faith better than the entire nation of Israel.

In a previous lesson, we talked about the Gentile woman that Jesus helped. Do you remember her? *(Refresh students' memories if not)* **(Matthew 15:21-29)** She and the Roman Centurion had something in common. She didn't expect Jesus to actually touch her daughter, and the Roman Centurion knew that Jesus didn't have to touch his servant. *They knew that if Jesus simply spoke the* *word, both the daughter and servant would be healed.* Because of this, Jesus said that they both had more faith than all of the people in Israel. Why? Because they had faith in the *spoken word* of Jesus!

Here's another question: Do we have enough faith to speak the word in prayer for someone, or do we feel that we have to *touch* them in order to use our faith?

(Get lamp) Let's think about electricity and how it works. What is the difference between the electricity we use to power this lamp and the electricity in lightning? Both produce light. Which is stronger? Lightening can travel through air, but the electricity used for this lamp must have wires to carry it to the bulb *(plug in the lamp)*. Without the wires, the electricity has no way to get to the bulb in order to light it! However, the electricity in lighting will light up the sky without need of a light bulb. Do you have "lightning faith" or "light bulb faith?" Is your faith strong enough to be transmitted simply by your words, or does it require your touch?

The Bible talks about great multitudes (or many people) coming to Jesus 11 different times for healing. Do you think He laid His hands on every single person? It is very doubtful, because it would have taken hours to do that; when would He have had time to teach? All that Jesus needed to do was speak, and many were healed! **(Matthew 4:24; 8:16; 12:15; 14:14; 15:30; 19:2; 21:14; Mark 1:34; 3:10; Luke 5:15; 6:17-19)**

In **Acts 5:15**, Peter's faith was so big that when his shadow moved across someone as he was walking by, *they were healed.* Do you have the same Jesus living in your heart? If you have the Holy Ghost, you do! Do you have "tiny" faith, or do you have "mustard seed faith?" If you have mustard seed faith, you can speak, and it will happen! **(Matthew 17:14-21; Luke 17:6)**

FAITH AND TRUST:
Are They the Same Thing?

Lesson suggestion: *Gather at least four eggs, a bowl or container, a chair, a large towel, and paper towels. Drain two eggs of their whites and yolk. You can accomplish this either one of two ways: (1) Make two small holes (one on each end) and simply blow air into the egg forcing the contents out the other hole, or (2) Make one small hole in one end of the egg and shake the contents out of the egg. You may want to mark the "full" eggs so that you can easily tell them apart!*

Many of us can quote **Hebrews 11:1:** *"Now faith is the substance of things hoped for, the evidence of things not seen.* **Verse 2** says, *"For by it the elders obtained a good report."* **(KJV)** Let's look at these verses in another translation. *"What is faith? It is the confident assurance that what we hope for is going to happen. It is the evidence of things we cannot yet see. God gave his approval to people in days of old because of their faith."* **(NLT)** How can we be sure that what we hope for will happen? The Bible tells us that if we want be saved, we *must* have faith in God.

Sometimes the word "faith" is difficult to understand because we don't use it every day. This is why we are also going to look at the word *"trust."* If we were to look in a dictionary, we would find that it means *"firm belief in the character, ability, strength, or truth of someone or something b: a person or thing in which confidence is placed"*[51] That sounds a lot like the Biblical definition of "faith." The two words are very much alike.

We are going to "cook up" some faith. I need one helper! Now, do not volunteer unless you *trust* me. It could get messy! *(Place the towels over the shoulders of the helper to protect his/her clothes.)* Hold this bowl while I crack these eggs.

Object Lesson: Crack at least two "good" eggs to cement the thought into their minds that all of the eggs are real and not cooked. While doing this, ask the child if they still trust you and asking if you can crack one above their head. Talk about how sticky the egg is or "crack" a few egg jokes. Ask them "If the white of the egg is called the albumin, what do we call the yellow part of the egg?" Answer: "The yolk." Without warning, take one of the empty shells and crush it directly above the helper.

(Child's name) placed his/her trust in me. He/She had faith that I would not mess up his/her clothes by getting egg on them. "*(Child's name)*, be honest, did you at any time wonder if you were going to get egg all over your head? I have one more egg left. Do you trust me to crack it over your head, or do you want me to crack it over the bowl?" (Crack the egg where the child directs. Choose the next part of your lesson according to how they choose.)

Over the head
(Child's name) trusted that I would not ruin *(his/her)* clothes. This is how we should view Jesus. He is much more trustworthy, or worthy of your faith, than I. I am a *(man/woman)*. One day, no matter how hard I try, I will eventually do something that will let you down. I am not perfect like Jesus. He will never let you down. You can always trust (or have faith in) Him.

In the Bowl
(Child's name) knows that I am human. *(He/She)* knows that there is a chance, no matter how hard I try, that I could have made a mistake and chose the wrong egg. *(He/She)* decided to be safe and make sure that *(his/her)* clothes were not ruined. There is no reason that we should look at Jesus that way. He will never let us down. Jesus will always do what is best for us. You can always trust, or have faith in Him. *(Send child to his/her seat with a "thank you.")*

---

[51] Merriam-Webster.com. Merriam-Webster, n.d. Web. 22 Oct. 2014. <http://www.merriam-webster.com/dictionary/trust>.

Let's read **Mark 12:41-44**: *"As Jesus sat facing the temple offering box, he watched how much money people put into it. Many rich people put in large amounts. A poor widow dropped in two small coins, worth less than a cent. He called his disciples and said to them, "I can guarantee this truth: This poor widow has given more than all the others. All of them have given what they could spare. But she, in her poverty, has given everything she had to live on."* (GW)

This widow gave everything that she had. She trusted God to meet her every need. God will always honor someone who has absolute faith in Him. Do you remember reading **Hebrews 11:1-2** at the start of this lesson? These people gained God's approval (acceptance) because of their faith in Him.

1 Kings 17:8-16 says, *"Then the LORD said to Elijah, Now go to the town of Zarephath, near Sidon, and stay there. I have commanded a widow who lives there to feed you. So Elijah went to Zarephath, and as he came to the town gate, he saw a widow gathering firewood. Please bring me a drink of water, he said to her. And as she was going to get it, he called out, And please bring me some bread, too. She answered, By the living LORD your God I swear that I don't have any bread. All I have is a handful of flour in a bowl and a bit of olive oil in a jar. I came here to gather some firewood to take back home and prepare what little I have for my son and me. That will be our last meal, and then we will starve to death. Don't worry, Elijah said to her. Go on and prepare your meal. But first make a small loaf from what you have and bring it to me, and then prepare the rest for you and your son. For this is what the LORD, the God of Israel, says: The bowl will not run out of flour or the jar run out of oil before the day that I, the LORD, send rain. The widow went and did as Elijah had told her, and all of them had enough food for many days. As the LORD had promised through Elijah, the bowl did not run out of flour nor did the jar run out of oil."* **(GNT)**

This woman and her son were about to eat their last meal; then, they would starve to death. Can you imagine what was going through her mind? Elijah had just asked that she give him *their last meal*. Should she trust the man of God? Should she tell him to leave? Not only was he asking for *her* last meal, but also *her son's* last meal. Notice: she did not even claim Elijah's God as her own. She was taking a huge step! However, by trusting Elijah and his God, she saved all of their lives! What would you have done? Could you have trusted (or had faith in) God in this situation?

You see, these words really are related. If you do not have faith in someone, you also do not trust them. However, if you trust someone, you automatically have faith in both them *and* what they say.

Do you trust, or have faith in, God? You should. He will always do what is best for you!

PRAYING FOR OTHERS:
The Laying on of Hands: How, Why, and When

> *Author's note to Teacher: It is not our intent of be legalistic in this area. As your children mature spiritually, they will desire to use their anointed prayers just as we do. As in any other area of life, children need boundaries to ensure unity and limited disruptions in the movement of the Spirit during your services; they also need encouragement for positive spiritual growth.*
>
> *Note from the author: We strongly suggest that you discuss this lesson with your pastor prior to teaching it. He may desire to add to, or take away from, these guidelines. As there are no scriptures included in the last section, we readily admit that these guiding principles are not "doctrine"; however, they were the ones approved by our pastor and proven by their use.*

I'm sure you've noticed the different things that ministers do when someone asks for prayer at the altar (the different ways that they pray for them). Are there any guidelines (rules) that we should follow when praying for someone? There are several reasons why we lay hands on someone, and this is what we're going to talk about today! I know we all want to be correct in our actions, so let's look at this a little closer and see what the Bible says.

Blessing

We find examples of blessings given by the laying on of hands. In **Genesis 48:9-20**, when Jacob was about to die, Joseph asked him to bless his sons, Ephraim and Manasseh. The Jews had a custom: at the end of their lives, the father (or grandfather) would lay their hands upon their sons (or grandsons) and pronounce a blessing over them. We see Jesus continuing this in the New Testament when, in **Matthew 19:13-15** and **Mark 10:15-16**, He blessed the children that were brought to Him.

Healing

Jesus often laid His hands on people when He healed them. We find examples of this in the following scriptures: **(Matthew 8:2-3, 14-15; Mark 5:23, 41; 6:4-5; 8:23-25; Luke 13:10-13)**. In **Acts 9:10-17**, Ananias went to Saul (Paul) to tell him how to be saved. First, before he did anything else, he laid his hands upon Saul and prayed that he would receive his sight. In **Acts 28:7-8**, we find that Paul followed Ananias' example when he laid his hands on Publius' father and prayed for his healing.

While praying with those wanting the Holy Ghost

We also find examples that tell of the apostles laying hands on people when praying for them to receive the Holy Ghost **(Acts 8:17; 9:17-15; 19:1-6)**.

Receiving a "gift of the Spirit"
In **1 Timothy 4:13** and **2 Timothy 1:4,** Paul encouraged Timothy to use a spiritual gift that he had received when hands were laid upon him.

As you can see, the Bible encourages us to pray for others. We should always follow in the examples of the Apostles. Unfortunately, the Bible did not spell out a list of "dos and don'ts" that tells us *how* we should pray for others. Because of this, we must rely on the common sense that God gave us. Let's look at some guidelines that will help us be more effective when we praying for others.

When can I pray for someone?

It is okay for you to pray with someone to receive the Holy Ghost. The best place for someone to feel the freedom to surrender to Jesus is when they are surrounded by praise and worship.

You may pray for someone who is being anointed for healing. God inhabits the praises of His people. Just think of how much you can boost someone's faith by your praise and worship!

You can pray for friends at the altar. You should always be ready to pray for your friends. They need your prayer and support.

When should I not pray for someone?

You should not interrupt if someone seems to want to pray alone. There are times when someone needs to talk to God about things that they don't want others to hear. If they act as if they want to be alone, please be thoughtful of their desire for privacy.

You should not bother someone by being insincere and laughing, etc. with other friends in the altar area. Just as you can create a place for God to touch others by your praise and worship, you can also destroy that atmosphere by talking or playing around someone who is praying. What would go through your mind if you walked into a room where your friends were talking and laughing? You would wonder what was funny, wouldn't you? Because we have the same effect on those that are praying, we need to be polite and respect their time of prayer. This is called reverence.

What can I do when I pray for someone?

Touch someone only on the arm or shoulder, but not the head. You see ministers do this; however, they are given authority by God to do so. In many places, touching someone's head means that you feel you are in authority over them.

If you are a boy, you may pray for a boy by touching them on the arm or shoulder. If you are a girl, you may pray for a girl by touching them on the arm or shoulder. This removes the possibility of your distracting them, or by causing them to think that you are assuming authority over them.

If you are a boy, you should never touch a girl when praying for them. If you are a girl, you should never touch a boy when praying for them. Again, you may see adults touch others. However, if you observe very closely, you will usually not see a man touch a woman anywhere but on her head or shoulder; the women should do the same. To touch anywhere else would not be appropriate. A touch may be embarrassing and very distracting (e.g. Boys, if you have a girlfriend and she comes to pray with you, would you be thinking about her, or Jesus?).

What should I not do when I pray for someone?

(Teachers: Have some fun with this; use your students to demonstrate the examples.)

Do not jerk them around. Be courteous; they are talking to Jesus! If someone were to jerk your arm, your mind would immediately begin wondering why your arm was jerked. Is someone trying to get your attention?

Don't shake them. One person was unable to receive the Holy Ghost for a year because another person who consistently prayed for him *also* consistently shook him around! This would frustrate the person praying because all he could think about the fact that he was being shaken!

Be careful where you place your hands. Another person finally received the Holy Ghost after seeking for it for a very long time. When asked why it took so long, he answered, "I had to get it tonight! You were about to tickle me to death!" You see, he was very ticklish! Every time someone would move his hand, it would tickle him and he would jerk. His sudden movement excited those praying for him, because they thought it was the Holy Ghost that was causing him to jerk around. This would then cause more movement, which caused even more tickling! He would eventually give up, becoming simply too exhausted (or tired) from being tickled so much.

Don't confuse the person for whom you are praying. If you are in a group praying for someone, there should always be a leader, and only that leader should give instructions to the person who is praying. Can you imagine the confusion caused by one person telling someone to "Hold on" and another telling them to "Let go!" Listening to two or more people is very difficult!

Don't pray loudly in someone's ear. If you need to pray loudly, do it away from their face and ear. They want the Holy Ghost, not a headache!

Please remember that our goal is to minister to others, and we do this by helping them get closer to God. If you feel directed by God to pray for someone, do it! If you feel the need to lay hands on someone, please be sure you *are* helping them, and that you *are* following these guidelines. The laying on of hands is important. However, that importance does not give us the right to be distracting when we do it.

Also, always remember that God loves you very much. He not only hears, but will answer, your prayers!

GIFTS OF THE SPIRIT, LESSON #1:
"Showing" Gifts

Lesson suggestion: Whiteboard, markers.

"Showing" Gifts = Word of Knowledge, Word of Wisdom, Discerning of Spirits

In one of our past lessons, we learned how our life could be like an ice cream sundae. It is up to us whether our life "tastes good" to God or not! We talked about the fruits of the Spirit: love, joy, peace, longsuffering, gentleness, goodness, faith, meekness, and temperance (or self-control). **(Galatians 5:22, 23)** We also introduced you to the gifts of the Spirit: word of knowledge, word of wisdom, discerning of spirits, gift of faith, gift of healing, gift of miracles, diverse (or different) kinds of tongues, interpretation of tongues, and the gift of prophecy. **(1 Corinthians 12:8-10)** We are going to take the next couple of weeks and learn more about these gifts, and about how God will S-T-R-E-T-C-H us spiritually when He finds us faithful!

God gives these gifts to Christians to prove that He is alive and that He has power over everything. Before we talk about the gifts, we need to explain some basic rules that apply to the gifts.

1. **God will never ask someone to do or say anything that disagrees with the Bible.** (**2 Timothy 3:16-17 BBE**) *"Every holy Writing which comes from God is of profit for teaching, for training, for guiding, for education in righteousness: So that the man of God may be complete, trained and made ready for every good work."*
2. **The Bible teaches us that God is always proper and orderly in His actions. We should follow His example. (1 Corinthians 14:37-40 GW)** *"Whoever thinks that he speaks for God or that he is spiritually gifted must acknowledge that what I write to you is what the Lord commands. But whoever ignores what I write should be ignored. So, brothers and sisters, desire to speak what God has revealed, and don't keep anyone from speaking in other languages. Everything must be done in a proper and orderly way."*
3. **Always be obedient to those who have authority over you. Having a special gift from God never allows someone to go beyond the authority of his or her leaders** (e.g., having a gift does not allow a child to disobey their parents or teachers). **(Hebrews 13:17 GW)** *"Obey your leaders, and accept their authority. They take care of you because they are responsible for you. Obey them so that they may do this work joyfully and not complain about you. (Causing them to complain would not be to your advantage.)"*
4. **God will not ask you to hurt someone.** Previously, we learned that **Galatians 5:22, 23** lists "gentleness" as one of the fruits of the Spirit.

We are going to split these gifts into three groups, which will help all of us remember them more easily: **"Showing," "Telling,"** and **"Doing."** Each gift is grouped by the way God uses each one to work in our lives.

In this lesson, we will learn about the "Showing" gifts. When God gives us one of these gifts, He chooses to "show" us things that we would not normally know. When He *does* show us something, we need to always go to someone in authority (like Pastor) and ask them how to use this information. This is important because: (1) Sometimes, God wants us to share what we know; (2) Sometimes, God shows us something only because He trusts us to simply <u>pray</u> about it and not say anything to anyone else. God never wants us to use what He shows us to hurt another person. Let's look at each of these more closely.

Word of Knowledge
This is special information that comes only from God about someone or something. These are facts that you could not know any other way except by God telling you. These are not guesses based upon things you already know. This comes directly from God, and is why it is so important that we know God's voice.

Examples
- In **Acts 5:1-11,** God gave Peter a word of knowledge that showed him the lie told by Ananias and Sapphira.
- While writing the book of The Revelation of Jesus Christ (the last book in the Bible), the Apostle John was given a word of knowledge about the seven churches of Asia. He had been exiled for several years on the island of Patmos, so there was no way for him to know the spiritual condition of these churches. God told John what to write in the letters that he was to send to them. **(Revelation 2-3)**

Word of Wisdom
God gives us a special ability to use the facts that we know. This is not what we call "common sense," although people who don't believe in the gifts of the Spirit (or God) may try to call it such. It goes beyond a learned ability to reason things out (or think things through).

Examples
- In **1 Kings 3:16-28**, two women come to Solomon. They lived in the same house, and both of them had recently given birth to a baby (we'll call them Mothers #1 and #2). While sleeping one night, Mother #2 accidentally rolled over on top of her baby and killed it. When she noticed what had happened, Mother #2 switched her dead child with Mother #1's child, while that mother was still sleeping, and then lied about it. Mother #1 wanted Solomon to decide which of them was the real mother of the living child. God gave Solomon the wisdom that helped him make the right decision.
- In **Luke 20:21-25**, the religious leaders tried to trick Jesus by trying to get Him to give his opinion on the issue (or argument) of paying taxes. The Romans required the Jews to pay taxes, but the Jews did not *like* to pay them. If Jesus had told them to ignore paying their taxes, the Romans would have arrested Him! If He had told them to pay taxes, the Jews would have hated Him. The wisdom in His answer, "Give to Caesar what belongs to Caesar, and give to God what belongs to God," caused them to leave Him alone.

Discerning of Spirits
God gives us the ability to know the spirit(s) that are at work in a situation. There are two types of spirits that work against God's purpose: human and demonic (of Satan). If we know which one is at work in a situation, we will know how to react. We often give Satan credit for our problems when he isn't even close by! Remember, Satan is not like God, so he cannot be everywhere at the same time. Therefore, most of our battles are with the human spirit.

Examples
- **Human:** In **Acts 8**, we find a man in Samaria named Simon who had been a magician before he became a believer. He wanted to "buy" the ability to give people the Holy Ghost. Peter told him to repent, because he realized that Simon had a greedy and bitter human spirit. **(Acts 8:18-23 BBE)** *"Now when Simon saw that the Holy Spirit was given through the touch of the Apostles' hands, he made them an offering of money, saying, Give me this power, so that when I put my hands on anyone he may get the Holy Spirit. But Peter said, May your money come to destruction with you, because you had the idea that what is freely given by God may be got for a price. You have no part in this business, because your heart is not right before God. Let your heart be changed, and make prayer to God that you may have forgiveness for your evil thoughts. For I see that you are prisoned in bitter envy and the chains of sin."*

- **Demonic:** We find Paul dealing with a demonic spirit in **Acts 16:16-18**: *"One day as we were going to the place of prayer, we were met by a young servant woman who had an evil spirit that enabled her to predict the future. She earned a lot of money for her owners by telling fortunes. She followed Paul and us, shouting, These men are servants of the Most High God! They announce to you how you can be saved! She did this for many days, until Paul became so upset that he turned around and said to the spirit, In the name of Jesus Christ I order you to come out of her! The spirit went out of her that very moment."* **(GNT)** Paul spoke to the spirit and commanded it to leave.

Next week, we will study the other two groups and learn other ways that God can use us to help build His Kingdom. Before we go, it is important to remember the guidelines we mentioned at the beginning.

1. *God will never tell you something that disagrees with the Bible.*
2. *God wants us to be correct in our actions.*
3. *Always be obedient to those who have authority over you.*
4. *God will not ask you to hurt someone.*

These gifts are available to us as we grow in our relationship with God. If we want Him to use us in this way, we need to prepare our hearts to be ready!

GIFTS OF THE SPIRIT, LESSON #2:
"Telling" and "Doing" Gifts

Lesson suggestion: Whiteboard, markers.

"Telling" Gifts = Diverse Kinds of Tongues, Interpretation of Tongues, Gift of Prophecy

"Doing" Gifts = Gift of Faith, Gift of Healing, Gift of Miracles

In our last lesson, we began by studying the **"Showing"** gifts of the Spirit. Remember, God uses these gifts to show us things we would not know otherwise. When we are faithful to Him, God feels comfortable in S-T-R-E-T-C-H-I-N-G us spiritually. Today we are going to look at the **"Telling"** and **"Doing"** gifts.

Before we go any further, let's review the guidelines we mentioned at the beginning:

1. *God will never tell you something that disagrees with the Bible.*
2. *God wants us to be correct in our actions.*
3. *Always be obedient to those who have authority over you.*
4. *God will not ask you to hurt someone.*

Let's get started!

"Telling" gifts

When God uses us through these three gifts, He is literally speaking through us. We speak *His* words! Remember, God will never have you say something that will hurt someone.

Diverse Kinds of Tongues
God gives us the ability to pray in tongues at any time. This is not the same as when someone speaks in tongues for the first time, as that is the sign (or signal) that one has received the Holy Ghost. While tongues is probably the most common gift, many people go through life rarely speaking in tongues. This does not mean that they are not saved; it simply means that they have never received the gift of diverse (or different) kinds of tongues. Paul talks about this gift in **1 Corinthians 14**. Following are two of the ways that God will use this gift.

<u>Examples</u>
- **Personally:** The person benefits by praying in tongues during their personal prayer time. Their prayer becomes God's prayer and God's words. Imagine how powerful your prayers become when you allow Him to pray through you! Depending on the type of prayer happening at any given moment, some people's "prayer language" even changes. For instance, if someone is worshiping in tongues, the language may be beautiful and song-like. If they are in a spiritual battle, their tongues may be strong and forceful. Paul tells us in **1 Corinthians 14:2**, *"Those who speak in strange tongues do not speak to others but to God, because no one understands them. They are speaking secret truths by the power of the Spirit."* **(GNT)**
- **To help others:** God may use a person with this gift to give a message to a group of people, such as a church congregation. When this happens, one should pray softly and listen to hear what God has to say to the group. God uses someone with the gift of interpretation to tell the group what was said in the message of tongues. The Apostle Paul tells us in **1 Corinthians 14:27-28**, *"If someone is going to speak in strange tongues, two or three at the most should speak, one after the other, and someone else must explain what is being said. But if no one is there who can explain, then the one who speaks in strange tongues must be quiet and speak only to himself and to God."* **(GNT)**

Interpretation of Tongues
God gives a person the ability to interpret an utterance of diverse kinds of tongues for the benefit of the group (as in a church service). We just read about this in **1 Corinthians 14:27-28**. It is important to be quiet and to listen to this message, as it is from God. It is important to understand the difference between two these two big words:

- ***Translation:*** *when someone states, in a language that the majority of a group understands, what was said during a message in tongue; it is usually word-for-word*
- ***Interpretation:*** *when someone explains the meaning of the tongues in an understandable language*

Paul used the word "interpret" [*to explain or tell the meaning of: present in understandable terms <interpret dreams> <needed help interpreting the results>*[52]]. **(1 Corinthians 14:27)** This is important, because it explains why both the message in tongues and the interpretation can be either long or short.

Gift of Prophecy
Having the gift of prophecy means that God has given you the ability to convey (or deliver) God's word, or to reveal God's word for the future. This gift can be used to warn (or to encourage) a person (or a group) about their relationship with God. God may also use a person with this gift to tell of events that will happen in the future. We find many examples of this in the Bible. In **Acts 21**, Paul was on his way to Jerusalem for the Passover. While meeting with several friends along the way, multiple prophecies were given that said he would be in danger if he continued his trip. It is interesting to note that Paul did not change his God-directed course; instead, the prophecy prepared him for what would take place in the near future.

"Doing" gifts

These gifts require us to be active, as they are often called the "power" gifts. Some people may feel that they are more powerful because the *results* are more visible; however, this is not the case. The most powerful gift is the one needed at any particular moment. Let me explain by asking you a question. If your family is driving down a busy highway and a big truck is coming toward you in your lane, what gift would be the most powerful right then? The gift of miracles, because you need rescued! You are in great danger! Let's look at another example: Your friend comes to you with a problem. They have a really big decision to make, and they don't know what to do. Would the gift of miracles be very powerful (or useful) at that moment? No; you would need the gift of wisdom.

We usually find that these "doing" gifts work together as a group. For example, if you do not have the gift of faith, it is doubtful that you will pray for a miracle.

Gift of Faith
When God gives you this gift, He gives you the ability to believe in God's power. He also gives you the ability to help others believe in it, too! A person with this gift is able to pray for great things and expect that they will happen. One example of great faith is found in **Joshua 10:12-13**. The children of Israel were fighting the Amorites, but it was almost evening and the battle was not over. Joshua did not want the Amorites to be able to escape during the night, so he commanded the sun and the moon to stand still until the battle was over. God rewarded his faith and what Joshua commanded actually happened! **(Acts 3:1-8) (Acts 14:8-10)**

Gift of Healing
God gives a person the ability to lay hands on (or pray for) someone, with healing being the result. Again, there are many examples of this in the Bible. An example of this would be the miracle, written about in **Acts 3:1,** immediately following the Day of Pentecost. Peter and John were on their way to the Temple to pray when they saw a lame man begging at the gate of the Temple. Although Peter and John

---

[52] "Interpret." *Merriam-Webster.com.* Merriam-Webster, n.d. Web. 11 Aug. 2014. <http://www.merriam-webster.com/dictionary/interpret>.

told him that they had no money, the lame man still expected something. They gave him something better than money; they prayed for him and he was healed! **(Acts 5:16; 8:7; 28:8)**

Gift of Miracles
God gives a person the ability to pray, believe, and see miracles happen. An example of this can be found in **II Kings 4:1-7**. A widow asked Elisha for his help, for her husband had died and they had many bills to pay. The creditors (or people she owed) were coming to make slaves of her sons in order to "make their money back." Elisha told the woman to borrow all of her neighbor's jars. Then, she was to fill the jars with the oil she had in a small bottle. Can you imagine her son's eyes when she took that *one small bottle of oil* and filled *many large jars* with it? **(2 Kings 6:1-7; Acts 6:8; 9:36-41)**

Remember, our first lesson about the gifts ended by saying that they are available to us as we grow in our relationship with God. If we want Him to use us this way, we need to prepare our hearts and ask for them.

God is very careful when He gives these gifts to someone. If you don't want any of these gifts, He won't force them on you. He also won't give you a gift that will hurt your spiritual growth. You see, although these gifts are special, you do not become a special "Super-Christian" when God gives you one. Let me explain. Many times in life, we consider someone special because of the things they own. The girl with the prettiest dress, or the boy with the newest gaming system, is treated differently because they have something that we want. This is not correct! The girl or boy is the same, with or without whatever it is that they have!

We must realize that when we receive a gift from God, it simply means that He has found us willing to allow Him to work through us. Our relationship with Him takes just as much effort. We still need to pray, read our Bible, and seek to stay as close to Jesus as we possibly can. He wants to shower us with His gifts, but He will only give them to us if He feels that we are able to use them properly.

WHAT DOES "GOD IS MY FATHER" MEAN?

Lesson suggestion: Whiteboard, markers. Optional: use a robe and ring when illustrating the return of the prodigal son.

The Bible tells us that God is our Father. Is He my Father? Is He your Father? Let's look at what the Bible says: **(Romans 8:14-16 KJV)** *"For as many as are led by the Spirit of God, they are the sons of God. For ye have not received the spirit of bondage again to fear; but ye have received the Spirit of adoption, whereby we cry, Abba, Father. The Spirit itself beareth witness with our spirit, that we are the children of God..."*

The Bible only talks about two men who never had an earthly father: Jesus and Adam.

There are three basic definitions for the word "father": (1) A male parent; (2) Someone who acts like the male parent; and (3) Creator or Originator. We know that God is our creator. That description is easy to understand. Did you know that He wants to fulfill the second definition, too? Yes, God wants to become *our spiritual parent.* Let's look at the verses a little closer and I will prove this to you.

Did you notice the strange word in verse 15 that came before the word Father? "Abba." Do you know what that means? Well, it means father, but it is more like "Daddy" (it expresses feelings or emotion). There is a love and a loyalty. Many more verses tell us that God is our Father.

You may ask, "Why is it important for me to know that God is my Father? What's in it for me?" Look at how the Bible describes our Heavenly Father in the following verses:

- **(Genesis 1:1)** *God created the Heaven and the earth.*
- **(Revelation 1:11)** *He is the Alpha and Omega, the Beginning and the Ending.*
- **(Psalms 24:7-10)** *He is the King of glory.*
- **(Revelation 19:6)** *Omnipotent – He has all power.*
- **(Ephesians 1:8)** *He has all knowledge.*
- **(Psalm 50:12)** *He owns everything.*

How would you like it if your dad were a millionaire and could give you anything that you asked for, or wanted? Your heavenly Father is better than that! Do you remember what we just read? Then why does He not give us *everything* we ask for? I have asked Him for lots of money many times. Why did I not receive it? Just think. If someone gave me 1 million dollars, I could pay off my bills, buy a new car, buy nice clothes, and travel around the world...and the list goes on. If you had a million dollars, just think of the toys, video game systems, clothes, etc. that you could have.

That sounds like such a good thing, doesn't it? In **Luke 15:10-24**, we find a son who thought the same way. We call him the "Prodigal Son." **Read the scripture aloud.**

You see, Jesus loves us so much that He died on the cross for us. He knows what we will do if He gives us too much.

I want to focus on the father in this parable. He loved his son so much that he gave him what he asked for, even though the father knew that the son would waste the money that he was receiving. After his son left, the father waited for him, hoping he would realize his mistake and come home. The Bible does not say how long the son was away. But, as soon as the father saw him walking down the road towards the house, he ran to meet him! He was not angry; instead, he was happy that his son had come back home! The father kissed his son and put his best robe on him; he even put the family ring on his finger. The robe showed that the father was restoring him to the family, and the family ring gave him the right to make important business decisions on behalf of his father. Those two special things gave him authority! Then, to top it all off, the father threw a party for him!

Some of you may have wonderful relationships with your father, while some of you may have been disappointed or hurt by yours. Although I don't have a miracle to fix your situation, I can gladly tell you that your Heavenly Father will never let you down. He will always be with you. **Matthew 28:20** says, *"...lo, I am with you alway, even unto the end of the world. Amen."* **(KJV)** Remember **Psalm 23**? Although your Heavenly Father will not always take you out of your problems, He will be with you while you go through them.

Do you think of God as your Father? Because our earthly father is the only example that we have to learn from, we generally assume that God, our spiritual Father, will act just like him. Have you transferred the feelings that you have for your earthly father to God? Do you think that He will act like your earthly father?

Let's read **Matthew 7:7-11**. Often, a simple comment will cause us to hesitate to trust Jesus as our Father. *(Teachers: a personal reference, good or bad, will help the children relate.)* Maybe our father is very busy and doesn't seem to have very much time for us. Certainly, Jesus must be too busy listening to everyone's prayers to have time for us too, right? Let's see what the Bible says: **(Luke 12:6-7 KJV)** *"Are not five sparrows sold for two farthings, and not one of them is forgotten before God? But even the very hairs of your head are all numbered. Fear not therefore: ye are of more value than many sparrows."*

Your Heavenly Father is never too busy to have time for you. He is Omniscient *(knows everything)*, Omnipresent *(can be everywhere at once)*, and Omnipotent *(has all power)*. No matter what our problem is, or where we are when we are going through it, He will always be with us, will always listen to us, and always have the power to help us. Let's pray to our Heavenly Father and thank him for loving us. There is truly none like Him!

GODHEAD LESSON #1:
There is One God

Lesson suggestion: *Whiteboard, markers, and an odd number of pencils for an object lesson illustration. See the point titled "Coequal."*

Note from the author: The following lessons teach on the Godhead, more commonly known as "Oneness." Many apostolic children are attending schools that base their curriculum upon doctrinal beliefs inconsistent with biblical truth. Confusion occurs when our children are placed in such an environment prior to receiving oneness teaching.

It is our goal to provide you with doctrinal lessons that will assist you in building a foundation upon which your children can stand, answering the 'what, why, and how' questions regarding apostolic truths and beliefs.

We have the following suggestions when planning to teach this topic:
(1) Take more than one week per lesson while teaching on this topic, as the material will most likely stimulate many questions within your students' minds.
(2) As children 5-7 (and sometimes even 8) would have a very hard time understanding these concepts, it would be beneficial for you to split the ages accordingly. An alternative lesson or activity (such as a "review game") is always an option.

Most of you have heard the word "trinity." You also know that the Bible does not teach the idea of three persons in the Godhead, although you may not completely understand why. In the next three lessons, we are going to do our best to explain this to you so that you will know "why" you believe in One God! In this lesson, we are going to looking at the question, *"Who is God?"* As we do, you will find that there is only one God, and if you open your mind to Him, this will be easy to understand.

Today, we are going to prove that one of the Trinitarian beliefs is incorrect: that there are three coequal, co-eternal, co-substantial persons, and that it's a mystery that is impossible to explain. While the Trinitarians cannot successfully explain the idea of the trinity, the Oneness of God is easy to understand.

Before we go any further, I want to remind you of past lessons. Do we use the Bible when teaching you? *(Yes)* Do we only use one verse? *(No)* The Bible instructs us to have several "witnesses" when establishing any fact **(Matthew 18:16) (2 Corinthians 13:1)** *(e.g., talk about a courtroom. It is very hard to convict or prove innocence if there is only one witness; whereas, if there are two or more witnesses with the same testimony, the point becomes more believable.).* If someone cannot show you at least two verses that support what he or she believes, you should be very careful when accepting what they say.

What do they mean by coequal, co-eternal, and co-substantial?

The Trinitarians are saying that while there are three persons, each one has all power and authority. All three have been present forever, with no beginning, and each one is made up of the same space or substance. Can any of you explain how this is possible?

Coequal (*Two helpers needed; an odd number of pencils is needed*)

This idea states, for example, that each person (Father, Son, and Holy Ghost) has all power. I have a handful of pencils that will represent "all power." One person has all the pencils *(give the pencils to your first helper)*. The second person also has all the pencils *(take the pencils from the first helper and give them to the second one)*. Wait! Now the first person has no pencils, or no power! Let's try splitting the pencils between the two helpers. That doesn't work either; neither have all the pencils, and one person has more pencils than the other does. I know! Try both holding the pencils at the same time. Do they now have all the pencils? Can either one use a pencil for writing? *(No)* Just as two people cannot each have all the pencils, two beings cannot have all the power!

Co-eternal *(One male helper needed)*

This means that all (Father, Son, and Holy Ghost) were present at the same time, forever, and without beginning. Let's pretend that this is my son. My son is as old as I am. In fact, my son was never born; he has always been with me. Can you understand this? *(No)* In order for this to be my son, he would need to be part of my family, and it would be impossible for him to be as old as I am because I was first. We *know* when the Jesus, the man, was born, for **Matthew 1:18-25** tells us so!

Co-substantial *(One helper needed)*

This means that each (Father, Son, and Holy Ghost) takes up the same space *(ask a child to come to the front and stand beside you)*. Now, *(name of child)* and I are two persons. Can you think of any way that I can stand in the same place as *(he/she)* without moving *(him/her)*? *(Attempt to do so)* No! If we could do that, we would no longer be two people, but one person.

Can you see why they call it a mystery? I don't understand it, can you? Notice: I didn't use any Bible verses when I explained these ideas! This is unusual, isn't it! This is because the Bible does not support the idea of a trinity, so it doesn't contain any scriptures that talk about it.

What do we mean there is one God and no separation of persons?

The Bible teaches that God, the Creator of all things, robed himself in flesh as Jesus, lived on the earth in order to show (and prove) Himself to the Jews; then, He died for our sins on the cross. Following His death, Jesus was in the grave three days, and then He rose again. After being with His followers another forty days, Jesus ascended into Heaven. Then, on the "Day of Pentecost," He came to live in our hearts as the Holy Ghost.

Let's look at the Bible and see what it says about there being one God! *(Choose readers with Bibles; having the children do this will help them see how the Bible clearly states that God is one.)*

Deuteronomy 6:4; Isaiah 43:10-11; 44:8; Zechariah 14:9; Mark 12:29-32; Romans 3:30; 1 Corinthians 8:4-6; Ephesians 4:5-6; James 2:19; Colossians 2:4-9; 1 Timothy 2:5-6; Revelation 4:2

In these scriptures, we have read about seven different men who followed God's directions, and also said that there is one God (Moses, Isaiah, Zechariah, Mark, Paul, James, and John). The Jews agree with us that there is one God. To believe otherwise would be blasphemy to them! The dictionary says that blasphemy is *"an indignity offered to God by words or writing; reproachful, contemptuous or irreverent words uttered impiously against Jehovah."*[53] (More plainly said, blasphemy means to say bad things, or joke, about God.) The Old Testament punishment for blasphemy was death!

(Teacher: for ease in teaching the history portion of this lesson, we refer to the "pagan-turned-Christian leaders" as the "mixed-up leaders." For your reference only, these leaders are also known as the Post-Apostolic fathers.)

In 65 B.C. (B.C. =Before Christ), a Roman general by the name of Pompey conquered the Jews of Judea. This meant that the Jews had to obey both Roman leaders and Roman laws. In 70 A.D. (A.D. =Anno Domini = In the Year of our Lord; about 70 years after Jesus' birth), the Roman Caesar, Vespasian, got tired of fighting with the Jews all of the time, so he decided to conquer them "once and for all!" His son, Titus, attacked Jerusalem and eventually destroyed the whole city, including the temple. Since the temple was destroyed, it meant that Jerusalem was no longer the center of the Christian faith.

---

[53] Noah Webster's 1828 Dictionary of American English

A few years later, the new Roman emperor, Constantine, wanted to stop the fighting between the pagans and the Christians, so he decided to mix the two religions together (a pagan is someone who worships idols, or false gods). The religious leaders in Constantinople became Christians; however, they had also worshipped pagan gods. Because these "mixed-up leaders" had not served God very long, and did not know all that they should, they used philosophy (the thoughts of man) to try to mix new beliefs with old ones. They became all mixed up! This is when the idea of God being "more than one person" was born. The Trinitarian formula for baptism (Father, Son and Holy Ghost) wasn't used until <u>years</u> after the death of the last original apostle of Jesus (John was the last to die, around 100 AD).

In trying to explain the trinity today, people will use the writings of these pagan religious leaders rather than to the Bible. **2 Timothy 3:16-17** says, *"All scripture is given by the inspiration of God."* **(KJV)** *This* is why we started this lesson with the statement, "If someone cannot show you at least two verses that support what they believe, you should be very careful when accepting their word." This is important! We must look to the Bible for all of our answers! Man's wisdom comes *second* to the Word of God at all times.

I want to end with the following verse: **(Deuteronomy 6:4 KJV)** *"Hear, O Israel: The LORD our God is one LORD:"* If you were to ask a Jew to quote this verse, this is how they would likely say it: *"Hear, O Israel: The LORD our God, The LORD is One:"*

We will continue to learn about One God next week!

GODHEAD LESSON #2:
Jesus is God

Lesson suggestion: *Whiteboard, markers.*

In this lesson, we will continue to look at the question, "Who is God?" Last week, we found that there is only one God, and if you open your mind to Him, this will be easy to understand.

Today, we're going to prove that another one of the Trinitarian ideas is incorrect: that Jesus is the human name of one of three persons in the Godhead, the Son *(also called the Word)*, and He is eternally *(no beginning or ending)* begotten *(born)*. Again, this idea of the trinity is impossible to explain; however, the oneness of God is easy to understand.

Before we go any further, I want to remind you: If someone cannot show you at least two verses that support what he or she believes, you should be very careful when accepting their word.

What does "Jesus is eternally begotten" mean?

How can someone who had no beginning be born? Isn't that contradictory (or opposite)? *(Yes)* Do you know when you were born? If you have a birth date, you couldn't have been around (or existed, lived) forever! Now, is there any one here that is the same age as their father? *(No)* If you were begotten (born), then your father must have been alive before you. *(Are you confused?)*

Let's look at the Bible to see what we can explain:

- **Isaiah 9:6** tells us that a Son will be born.
- **Matthew 1:18-25** describes a conversation between Joseph and an angel foretelling the birth of Jesus. [*Foretell: v. to predict; to tell before an event happens; to prophesy.*[54]]
- **Luke 1:30-35** describes the conversations between the angel and Mary foretelling the birth of Jesus.
- **Galatians 4:4-6** reminds the church of the birth of Jesus.

These events happened about 2000 years ago. We know that Jesus had a beginning.

(Teacher: for ease in teaching the history portion of this lesson, we refer to the "pagan-turned-Christian leaders" as the "mixed-up leaders." For your reference only, these leaders are also known as the Post-Apostolic fathers.)

What do they mean when they say that Jesus, the Son, is the second person of the Godhead?

Trinitarians believe that the One God is made up of three persons: Father, Son, and Holy Ghost. The apostles never taught this. In fact, it was considered heresy (blasphemy or lies) until about 170 AD. Between the time of John's death (about 100 A.D.) and 170 A.D., the argument centered on a belief in *two* persons: Father and Son.

You see, the "mixed-up leaders" were trying to mix the Christian teachings with their pagan teachings. Christianity had become so popular that there were more Christians than there were pagans! Many pagans became Christian in name only, just so they could be part of the majority, or "the crowd." Because the "mixed-up leaders" did not have a true relationship with God, they tried to use their minds (human thinking/philosophy) to reason out (or explain) the differences between their pagan background and Christianity. Any time you rely on the wisdom of man, you will make mistakes!

---

[54] Noah Webster's 1828 Dictionary of American English

Again, let's look at the Bible. **Isaiah 9:6** describes Jesus using two phrases:

- *"The mighty God."* The Hebrew word used here is "El," and is the same word used in the Old Testament when talking about the Creator.
- *"The everlasting Father."* Wait! They just said He was the Son. How can He be two people at the same time? He can't! There is only one God.

It is important to understand two points:

- "Father" or Holy Ghost": we are referring to the Spirit of God.
- "Son": we are talking about the human part of Jesus.

John 1:1-14 talks about the Word being God, and how God became flesh. "Word" comes from a Greek word, "Logos," which means a "spoken or written word" (concept or idea). At the beginning of time, God already had the idea of coming to earth as Jesus; He knew that if He didn't come, we would never be able to live in a way that was pleasing to Him.

In **John 10:30-33**, Jesus was in the temple teaching and made the statement, *"I and my Father are one."* The Jews became so angry that they wanted to stone Him, because they understood Him to be saying, "I am God."

In **John 14:8-11**, Philip asks to be shown the Father. In **verse 9**, Jesus scolds him by asking, *"I have been with all of you for a long time. Don't you know me yet, Philip? The person who has seen me has seen the Father. So how can you say, 'Show us the Father'?"* **(GW)**

Colossians 2:9 states that the fullness of the Godhead dwelled in the body of Jesus Christ.

Remember, the Bible teaches that God robed himself in flesh and came to earth as Jesus. He was born of Mary (a virgin), and fulfilled every prophecy that was recorded in the Old Testament about the Messiah. Because He was born of Mary (a human), the *man* Jesus had a beginning. The Jews knew that the Messiah would be God in flesh. They also knew that there is only one God (and today's Jews still believe in One God). They were just unaccustomed (or unused) to feeling God's presence among them, which caused them to refuse to believe in Jesus as their Messiah! We *know* that He is the Messiah. Therefore, He must have been the one true God in flesh!

In our next lesson, we're going to learn why the name of Jesus is so important. Don't miss it!

GODHEAD LESSON #3:
Why is the Name of Jesus so Important?

Lesson suggestion: *Whiteboard, markers.*

For the past two lessons, we have been looking at the question, "Who is God?" So far, we have found that there is only one God, and if you open your mind to Him, this will be easy to understand. In addition, we know that God robed Himself in flesh, became the man Jesus, and came to earth to die for our sins.

Today, we're going to show that another one of the Trinitarians' ideas is incorrect: that Jesus is the human name of one of three persons in the Godhead, the Son (also called the Word), and that it should not be used in baptism. While this idea of the trinity can't be found in the Bible, we can easily prove the importance of the name Jesus.

Before we go any further, I want to remind you: If someone cannot show you at least two verses that support what he or she believes, you should be very careful in accepting their word.

Jesus stated that He was Jehovah several times in His ministry.

- In **Matthew 4:3**, while being tempted of Satan, Jesus quotes **Deuteronomy 6:16**. The word LORD in Deuteronomy is Jehovah. Jesus is saying that He is Jehovah in human form.
- In **John 8:58-59**, Jesus was talking with the Pharisees and said, *"Before Abraham was, I AM."* This made the Jews want to stone Him, because Jesus was saying that He was God. Do you remember the story of Moses and the burning bush? **(Genesis 3:13-16)** When God appeared to Moses in the burning bush, He told Moses to tell the Israelites that "I AM" sent him. Anyone who claimed to be God was guilty of the sin of blasphemy, and the punishment was stoning. Of course, God could say it and not blaspheme (or lie).

The Bible tells us that baptism should be in the name of Jesus. Peter taught it in **Acts 2:38**. The church obeyed in **Acts 8:12-16; 10:48; 19:5;** and **Acts 22:16**. Paul taught it in **Romans 6:3** and **Galatians 3:27**.

Have you ever heard of anyone being healed, or a devil being cast out, by the titles Father, Son, and Holy Ghost? *(No)* However, if you read the book of Acts, miracles were constantly happening when the name of Jesus was spoken. **(Acts 3:6; 9:34; 16:18)** Did you know that the only thing the priests wanted the apostles to stop doing was using the name of Jesus? **(Acts 4:18; 9:29)**

So, how did the Trinitarians get the idea of Father, Son, and Holy Ghost baptism? **Ephesians 4:5** states that there is one baptism. **Matthew 28:19** says, *"...baptizing them in the name of the Father, and of the Son, and of the Holy Ghost:"* Is this incorrect? Let's look at this verse using the rules God put in the Bible. How many witnesses do you need? **(Matthew 18:16)** You need at least two! Can you find anywhere in the Bible that "might" cause someone to wrongly believe that they should be baptized in the titles? *(No)* Does this mean the Bible is wrong? *(No)* You cannot have it both ways. If there is only one way to be baptized, which one is right?

Let's look at this verse a little closer:

- Jesus told us to baptize using *a name*. Are Father, Son, and Holy Ghost names? Let me explain it like this: I am a *(father/mother)* and a *(son/daughter)*. I also have Jesus living in me, because I have the Holy Ghost. I fill all three titles. Would it do you any good to be baptized in the name of "(teacher's name)?" *(No)* I did not die for your sins. My name will not take you to Heaven!

- Do you remember learning about the difference between singular (one) and plural (more than one) in school? Is the word "name" plural? *(No)* This means that Jesus was only talking about <u>one name</u>. What is that name? <u>JESUS</u>.

The apostles obeyed Jesus by baptizing in His name. Peter forcefully stated in **Acts 4:12,** *"...there is none other name under heaven given among men, whereby we must be saved."* **(KJV)** In **Romans 10:13**, Paul agreed with Peter by saying, *"...whosoever shall call upon the name of the Lord shall be saved."* **(KJV)**

Why do you think Satan wants to get away from "the name?" To understand this, let's look at why a name is important. How do you know that someone belongs to your family? You have the same name! My children have my name. I have my father's name, and my father has his father's name!

Think with me about something for just a minute. How do you feel when you are at home? (Comfortable; "at home") Now think about how it is when you are at a friend's house. Do you feel the same? *(No)* Why? Because it is not your home! You don't belong to (or aren't a part of) the family that lives there.

What happens when someone is adopted into a family? They are given the family name; they now belong to that family. This is what happens when you are baptized in Jesus' name. You are adopted into the family of God!

Not being baptized is kind of like visiting a friend's house. You get to eat when they eat, play when they play, and sleep when they sleep. However, you never quite feel at home. If you were to fall and hurt your knee, would you feel comfortable climbing up into the lap of your friend's father? (No, probably not) Why? He is not your father! You are not part of his family. You don't have the privileges of a family member!

If you haven't been baptized in Jesus' name, then He is not your father. Yes, He will take care of you as a friend would, but it is so much different when you are a part of His family. Satan knows this is true, and this is why he wants to keep you from becoming part of God's family. If you do not take on the name of Jesus, you are not a member of the family of God. If Satan can convince people to ignore Jesus' name in baptism, he can cause them to feel like they are "just visiting." They will never feel at home until they become a part of God's family.

Satan doesn't want you to understand that there really is just *one God*! He wants you to question the need for the name of Jesus, for he knows that if he is successful, he can keep you from becoming a part of God's family.

Teacher: we suggest having all three lessons available at the close of this lesson; then, make time to answer any questions that your students may have. It will allow you to recap any material not clearly understood, giving an opportunity to see the "gap areas" in your student's comprehension of the subject. If there are points not easily understood by many, we recommend a review.

PART III

Shame:

Origin
Symptoms
Deliverance

We have been sprinkled with his blood to free us from a guilty conscience, and our bodies have been washed with clean water. So we must continue to come to him with a sincere heart and strong faith. We must continue to hold firmly to our declaration of faith. The one who made the promise is faithful.

(Hebrews 10:22-23 GW)

A Ministerial Insight on Shame...

The importance of this lesson cannot be overemphasized because it is a long-lasting condition that affects nearly every facet of our being.

Shame is having a grudge against one's self. We became acquainted with it early in life when our parents scolded us with the harsh tones of "shame on you" after we had broken a rule, or spilled our milk through carelessness. The meaning thus carried heavy guilt because someone we loved, someone who was displeased with our actions, spoke it.

It would be easy to carry that same feeling all through life because we did something wrong and cannot forgive ourselves. The point is that *God does forgive us* when we transgress His Law; He gave us stripes on His back and sinless blood that, upon repentance, will cover our wrongdoing. If He paid for it, why should we carry guilt when it has already taken care of?

The Alphins do a commendable job of bringing the lesson within the grasp of a young mind (shame that someone else brings, and shame brought on by your own doing). It is so important that each student knows how much Jesus loves them, yet hates their sin.

This can and will be with them the rest of their lives (both positively and negatively), depending on how successfully the material is taught.

Be sure you understand these lessons ... it is imperative.

Rev. William L. Sciscoe, Bishop
The Church Triumphant of Columbus, Ohio

A Note from the Authors...

One may not understand the necessity of this topic being presented to children. However, we have personally experienced, and witnessed in others, how a life free from shame is one that can be better surrendered to Christ for service. Literally everyone in the world has suffered shame at some point in their lives, and it is not God's will that His children remain bound by it, as it can be completely crippling to one's walk with Him.

The next several lessons deal with the issue of shame: its conception, symptoms, and a plan for deliverance from it. *If you are teaching in a class setting, we highly recommend teaching this only to older students, as younger children will not be able to reconcile the issue of shame in their minds.*

We both became aware of issues in our own lives as we were taught about Shame at MannaFest meetings organized by Rev. Chester Wright (*Antioch, The Apostolic Church*, Annapolis, MD) and our Pastor, Rev. William L. Sciscoe. Glenda was blessed in that she was able to attend a series of sessions concentrating solely on the subject. The following lessons were derived from verbatim lecture notes taken during those meetings that were led by Rev. Chester Wright, Rev. William Sciscoe, Rev. Franklin Howard, Rev. D. Shatwell, and Rev. Danny Hood.

This subject demands continuity in attendance. It may be that you need to communicate with each of your students' parents to ensure that they are aware of this necessity. In addition, *we suggest not admitting new students after the start of lesson one*. This will remove the necessity of having to recap the entire concept of shame, thus allowing the other students to continue in the learning process. Obviously, these are lessons that can be taught at any time; should you have students that cannot attend the first session, you can plan another. *It is especially important that new students are not involved when teaching lesson four, as they will not comprehend either the subject or the purpose.*

In preparation for the final lesson, we recommend that adequate time for both instruction and prayer are made available. Invite experienced intercessors to attend who can pray with the children. It is also vital that these adults understand the concept of shame so that they will know how to help the children pray.

When preparing to re-teach the "Shame" lessons, include the students who have previously attended. We personally experienced multiple healings from shame after attending numerous sessions on the subject. Additionally, we have continued to apply the "forgive and release" process, both personally and through ministry to others. Our spiritual enemy continues to attack us on a constant basis, so seeking healing is an ongoing process. Having an attitude of forgiveness, both towards ourselves and others, ensures that God will continue to forgive us.

For more information on this subject, we suggest that you review the Shame studies, authored and compiled by Rev. Chester Wright, which provide an in-depth look at the subject of shame. It is a very real issue that affects everyone, both Christian and non-Christian alike. His materials illuminate one's thought process and spirit, thus bringing an anointed revelation of how to live a shame-free, overcoming Christian walk. We pray that these lessons open doors of healing in the lives of your students.

Mark and Glenda Alphin

Note to teacher: *these definitions are for reference and study purposes only, as they would be very difficult for a child to understand.* **Reworded definitions for your students' understanding are provided within the lessons as needed.**

- **Shame:** (n.) "A painful sensation excited by a consciousness of guilt, or of having done something which injures reputation; or by of that which nature or modesty prompts us to conceal."[55]

- **Shame:** (v.) "To make ashamed..."[56]

- **Dishonor:** (v.) "To disgrace; to bring reproach or shame on; to stain the character of; to lessen reputation."[57]

- **Dishonor:** (v.) "To treat with indignity."[58]

- **Ashamed:** (adj.) "Affected by shame; abashed or confused by guilt or a conviction of some criminal action or indecorous conduct, or by the exposure of some gross errors or misconduct, which the person is conscious must be wrong, and which tends to impair his honor or reputation."[59]

- **Confusion:** (n.) "Abashment; shame."[60]

- **Abash:** (v.) "To be confounded, or ashamed."[61]

- **Abashment:** (n.) "Confusion from shame."[62]

- **Wound:** (n.) "Injury; hurt; as a wound given to credit or reputation."[63]

- **Offended:** (pp.) "Displeased."[64]

- **Resentment:** (n.) "The excitement of passion which proceeds from a sense of wrong offered to ourselves, or to those who are connected with us; anger."[65]

- **Grudge:** (n.) "Sullen malice or malevolence; ill will; secret enmity; hatred; as an old grudge."[66]

- **Hate:** (v.) "To dislike greatly; to have a great aversion to."[67]

- **Bitterness:** (n.) "In a figurative sense, extreme enmity, grudge, hatred; or rather an excessive degree or implacableness of passions and emotions; as the bitterness of anger."[68]

- **Unforgiven:** (a.) "Not forgiven; not pardoned."[69]

---

[55] Noah Webster's 1828 Dictionary of American English
[56] Noah Webster's 1828 Dictionary of American English
[57] Noah Webster's 1828 Dictionary of American English
[58] Noah Webster's 1828 Dictionary of American English
[59] Noah Webster's 1828 Dictionary of American English
[60] Noah Webster's 1828 Dictionary of American English
[61] Noah Webster's 1828 Dictionary of American English
[62] Noah Webster's 1828 Dictionary of American English
[63] Noah Webster's 1828 Dictionary of American English
[64] Noah Webster's 1828 Dictionary of American English
[65] Noah Webster's 1828 Dictionary of American English
[66] Noah Webster's 1828 Dictionary of American English
[67] Noah Webster's 1828 Dictionary of American English
[68] Noah Webster's 1828 Dictionary of American English
[69] Noah Webster's 1828 Dictionary of American English

SHAME LESSON #1:
What is Shame?

Lesson suggestion: *Whiteboard, markers.*

Have you ever heard the expression "Shame on you?" What about, "I am so ashamed of you!" For the next few weeks, we are going to be talking about this. We will all experience shame at some point in our lives, and we need to know (1) what shame is, and (2) how to deal with it when it happens.

Since there are several different meanings for shame, we will be using a few of dictionary definitions during our lessons. We'll be sure to go slow so that you understand each of them clearly. Be sure to ask questions if you get confused!

Words like "shame," "dishonor" (disapproval), and "being ashamed" (feeling badly, disapproved of) are all part of the same word family. There are many different ways that shame can affect us, so let's look at a few examples of how shame can happen in someone's life.

1. **Your actions**
   - *A thing (or things) that you HAVE done* that you wish you could change (e.g., lying, stealing, cheating, etc.)
   - *Something that you SHOULD HAVE done* but didn't do (e.g., not telling the truth)
   - *Something happens that makes us feel guilty.* And, because we feel guilty, we decide to hide what occurred (or took place). This results in shame.
   - *Someone else makes you feel ashamed* (or feel bad), about something that either you were involved in, or that you did. When you have this kind of shame, it is also called dishonor (disapproval).

2. **Disappointing someone (yourself, mom and dad, others)**
   - *E.g., you do not study nearly enough* for a test (or forget about it altogether), which then causes bad grades on a report card. Your parents/guardian are upset and disappointed, which makes you feel badly because you knew you could have done better.
   - *When something happens that causes you to have shame, you then "feel ashamed."* Has anyone ever felt ashamed about something before? Let's look at this word and see what it means.
     - *To be ashamed means to feel bad about something.*

3. **Rejection by someone close to you**
   - *Dad and mom get divorced;* one parent leaves.
   - *Dad or mom is too busy to spend time with you;* you also don't get hugs as often as you should. You feel like they are too busy for you.
   - *Someone besides a* parent that you highly admire and respect disappoints or hurts you somehow.
   - *Someone accuses you* of doing something you did not do.
   - *When things happen that we do not understand, we can become confused.* If the confusion is not taken care of and explained, a misunderstanding takes place. The misunderstanding can then turn into shame.

4. **Mental or Emotional Abuse**
   - *Someone is consistently mean to you* over a long period of time (e.g., school bully hounding you every year; people are calling you stupid, dumb, etc.; the kids in your class at school make fun of you; your siblings are constantly picking on you; a teacher is unkind to you for no obvious reason).
   - *Someone saying to you* "Why can't you be like ... (someone else)?"

- *To be treated with indignity;* this means that someone says or does something to show dislike for you.

5. **Physical abuse**
    - A *person is violent with you* (shoving, hitting, punching, etc.)
    - *Someone is inappropriate* with you physically **(note to teacher: do not elaborate on this subject; statement is provided to student for information only.)**
    - *To disgrace or hurt the character of someone;* this means that someone does something to make you seem like a less important person; also, to make you "look bad."

It is likely that you have all experienced more than one of the things we have just discussed. *There are really two kinds of shame: (1) The shame that someone puts upon you, and (2) shame that you bring on yourself.*

We have talked about the ways shame can come into your life, and we've talked about definitions from the dictionary. What does the Bible say about shame?

First type of shame: Someone putting shame on someone else

King Saul brings shame to David. (1 Samuel 20:24) King Saul had become very jealous of David. He was certain that David would end up taking the kingdom from him. Because of this, he tried to kill David several times with a spear. King Saul's son, Jonathon, and David were very best friends. King Saul was having a festival at his palace, and David had not come to dinner for two days. The King became angry and questioned his son, Jonathon, about it. When Jonathon told him that David had gone to Bethlehem to offer sacrifices with his family, King Saul became very angry, and this is what he said: **(1 Samuel 20:30-34)** *"Son of a crooked and rebellious woman! he called Jonathan. I know you've sided with Jesse's son. You have no shame. You act as if you are your mother's son but not mine. As long as Jesse's son lives on earth, neither you nor your right to be king is secure. Now, send some men to bring him to me. He's a dead man! Jonathan asked his father, Why should he be killed? What has he done? Saul raised his spear to strike him. Then Jonathan knew his father was determined to kill David. Jonathan got up from the table very angry and ate nothing that second day of the month. He was worried sick about David because Jonathan had been humiliated by his own father."* **(GW)** [*Humiliated = shamed.*]

King Saul had accused David of wanting to replace both the King and Jonathon as king. This means that the King had accused him of planning to do something that David was _not_ planning to do! *This was not true, but because he spoke this aloud, it brought shame to David.* Additionally, King Saul did two things that put shame upon his son, Jonathan: (1) he showed disrespect to his wife, and Jonathan's mother, by calling her names, and (2) King Saul raised his spear against his own son. The King had a bad habit of saying hurtful things out of anger. When people do this, it puts shame on the ones to whom they are speaking.

Second type of shame: Someone bringing shame upon himself or herself

King Saul brings shame upon himself. King Saul went to battle against the Philistines. The Israelite army split up into different groups, with Jonathon leading one army and Saul leading another. **Read 1 Samuel 13:2** After Jonathon won his battle, Saul began to act prideful, saying "Look what *I've* done; *I've* beat them!" **Read 1 Samuel 13:3, 4.** When the Philistines heard this, boy, were they upset! They decided to go after King Saul in full force! King Saul realized that he was in big trouble, but it was too late! His army started getting nervous. To top it all off, the prophet Samuel was supposed to meet him at Gilgal in order to offer sacrifices, but he hadn't yet arrived! So, King Saul decided to offer sacrifices without Samuel. This was a problem, because the prophet Samuel had told Saul he would come down and offer a sacrifice offering for peace. **Read 1 Samuel 10:8.** Because Saul's heart was not as clean as it should be, he wasn't supposed to make a sacrifice himself. Not only that, when he performed the sacrifice, he disobeyed very important rules laid down for him when he anointed king!

<u>This disobedience brought shame upon him</u>; however, he did not repent. From that time on, he became more and more rebellious.

Remember, we said that there are two kinds of shame: (1) The shame that someone puts upon you, and (2) shame that you bring on yourself.

We now understand the meaning of shame. In our next lessons, we will learn what happens when we have it. Then, we will learn some very important things: (1) How to recognize what our shame is, and (2) how to get <u>rid</u> of it! Make sure you are here for the next several lessons; you won't want to miss the end!

SHAME LESSON #2:
How Shame Affects Our Relationships

Lesson suggestion: Whiteboard, markers.

We are continuing to talk about shame. Last week, we learned that there are *really two kinds of shame: (1) The shame that someone puts upon you, and (2) shame that you bring on yourself.* Today we are going to talk about how shame can affect our emotions: how we view what others feel about us, and how we feel about ourselves.

There are three basic relationships in our lives.

1. Our relationship with **God**.
2. Our relationship with **others**.
3. Our relationship with **ourselves**.

The relationship that we want to focus on right now is the one that we have with ourselves. It is important that we are able to love ourselves! I am not talking about being prideful in how we look. I am talking about how we feel about ourselves. Do you love yourself? Do you believe that you are a good person? You see, if we do not love ourselves, it will be impossible for us to believe that God will love us. And, if we can't love ourselves, we won't let God love us because we won't feel worthy of His love.

Mark 12:30-31 says, *"Love the Lord your God with all your heart, with all your soul, with all your mind, and with all your strength.' The second most important commandment is this: 'Love your neighbor as you love yourself.' There is no other commandment more important than these two."* **(GNT)** Notice: He says, *"Love your neighbor as you love yourself."* It is impossible for us to love others if we don't love ourselves!

You see, we *must* be very important to Jesus, because He died for us. Why would He do that if He did not love us? Would you put yourself in a situation like that for someone that you did not love? (Discussion) **1 John 3:16a** says, *"We understand what love is when we realize that Christ gave his life for us."* **(GW)** He died for you and for me. God's love for us is greater than anyone else's could ever be!

He does not love us for what we do; He loves us for who we are. **Romans 8:31b** says, *"If God be for us, who can be against us?"* **(KJV)** It is nearly impossible for us to love others if we do not love ourselves!

There are three things that we must do.

1. "We must allow God to enable us to love Him.
2. We must allow God to love others through us.
3. It is vitally important that we allow God to help us love ourselves."[70]

Our problems begin when (1) we are hurt (or wounded) by our failures, or (2) when others reject us. We allow our hurts to take root in our heart, which allows a place for the devil to come and visit. Satan will lie to us and cause us to believe that we are unlovable. It is not true, but in the midst of feeling bad, it becomes all that we can see and believe about ourselves.

If we do not ask God to heal our hurt, it can turn into bitterness. Bitterness happens when we do not forgive someone; it's an emotion that can cause resentment, a grudge, and even hate!

---

[70] "Shame Book Series (The Shame Notebook), Book 2: "What is Shame?" Antioch Publishes the Word 2001, Rev. Chester Wright.

Resentment means to feel as though someone did something wrong to us, or to be angry. When we have a grudge, it means we have bad feelings towards someone else. To hate is to dislike someone greatly (or a lot). **Ephesians 4:26-27** says, *"Don't get so angry that you sin. Don't go to bed angry and don't give the devil a chance."* **(CEV)** We should not give the devil a chance to lie to us!

What will happen if we refuse to forgive?

1. *If we do not forgive ourselves, and others, it can cause harm to our relationship with God. Holding a grudge will put imaginary chains on our faith and will stop God from being able to answer our prayers. It can also cause God to ignore our prayer for forgiveness.* **Read Mark 11:24-26** and **Matthew 6:9-15** *(a different version than KJV may be helpful)*. [Trespass: (n.) "Any injury or offense done to another."[71]]

   When we repent, God covers our sins with His blood. Holding a grudge will also remove the blood from those sins that God has already forgiven. Not forgiving others is the only sin that will cause God to do this. **Read Matthew 18:21-35.**

2. *Continuing to hold a grudge, or not forgive, will give Satan a chance to bother us all of the time.* **Read 2 Corinthians 2:10-11.**

3. *No matter who my grudge is against (God, others, or myself), it can do the same amount of damage.* [Damage: (v.i.) "To receive harm."[72]]

When we believe Satan's lies, it causes us to choose between two directions for our life.

- We believe that God can't forgive us of our sins; this causes us to give up even trying to live for Him.
- We continue to serve God the best that we can, although we really can't do more than just "go through the motions" of serving Him because we are carrying so much shame around.

We must believe that God loves us with an unfailing love. No matter what we do, say, or think, He will never stop loving us. This will help us get to the place where we can be healed from our hurts. We must call upon God for help! David had many troubles in his life, and he never hesitated to call upon the Lord when he needed Him. **(Psalm 55:1-5 NLT)** *"Listen to my prayer, O God. Do not ignore my cry for help! Please listen and answer me, for I am overwhelmed by my troubles. My enemies shout at me, making loud and wicked threats. They bring trouble on me, hunting me down in their anger. My heart is in anguish. The terror of death overpowers me. Fear and trembling overwhelm me. I can't stop shaking."*

(Psalm 39:12 NLT) *"Hear my prayer, O LORD! Listen to my cries for help! Don't ignore my tears."*

(Psalm 40:1-3 NLT) *"I waited patiently for the LORD to help me, and he turned to me and heard my cry. He lifted me out of the pit of despair, out of the mud and the mire. He set my feet on solid ground and steadied me as I walked along. He has given me a new song to sing, a hymn of praise to our God."*

Let's take a few minutes to talk to Jesus. Ask Him to help you completely understand the things that you have heard. If we can learn these things now, it will save us many disappointments and hurts as we grow older.

We have learned what shame is, and we have learned how it can affect our relationships. Next week, we will learn how shame can mess up our life, if we allow it to do so. Make sure that you're here; you don't want to miss out!

NOTES

---

[71] Noah Webster's 1828 Dictionary of American English
[72] Noah Webster's 1828 Dictionary of American English

SHAME LESSON #3:
How Can Shame Mess Up Our Lives?

Lesson suggestion: *Whiteboard, markers.*

Remember, we said that there are two kinds of shame: (1) The shame that someone puts upon you, and (2) shame that you bring on yourself. Now that we have learned what shame is, we're going to learn how the devil can use it against us. When we carry shame around with us, it is like a flashing neon sign to Satan that says, "I'm available."

The devil is the worst enemy that each one of us could possibly have, because he will do whatever he can to pull us away from God. He will take a bad situation and make it much, much worse. How do we know this? The Bible says that the devil walks about like a roaring lion, looking for someone to devour (or eat). **(1 Peter 5:8)** Now, this doesn't mean that he will really eat you; it simply means that he wants to destroy you. Satan's goal is to ruin your spiritual life (your walk with God); however, when this happens, it nearly always affects your physical life (by sickness, problems with family, etc.).

You may ask, *"What did I ever do to the devil?" "Why is he so interested in me?"* The devil's biggest goal is to pull you away from God. Satan has had a grudge against God ever since the Lord kicked him out of heaven. **(Luke 10:18; Isaiah 14:12-14)** Then, when Adam and Eve messed up in the garden, Satan was cursed to crawl on his belly. **Read Genesis 3:1-15.**

God placed an eternal curse on Satan that would cause him to crawl on his belly, the lowest place on earth, and man would forever be able to step on his head. The only chance he has to save himself is to fight back! The devil knows that Jesus died so that you might have eternal life. However, he also knows that God will not make you serve Him. He gives you the choice to do so! **(Matthew 7:13-14; 16:24)**

Remember, we're talking about shame, and why the devil does all he can to use it against us. The next questions are, *"How does he use it? What does he do with it? How can he make me stumble in my walk with God because I have shame?"*

When a situation occurs that brings about shame, we must do several things to resolve (take care of) it:

1. If we have done something wrong, we must repent and forgive ourselves for what we did.
2. If someone has done something to us, we must forgive him or her.

When we do not do either of these two things, the shame seeps into our heart and becomes part of us.

In your mind, create a picture of a sidewalk that hasn't been repaired for a very long time. The concrete is old and cracked. No one has cared enough to come back and fill in the holes. This is what shame does to us; it leaves cracks in our spiritual sidewalk, and all the devil has to do is hop right through them! Usually, though, Satan doesn't hop right in; he enters slowly, so you don't realize he's there at first.

Remember, we're talking about shame. What are the two types of shame? (1) The shame that someone puts upon you, and (2) shame that you bring on yourself.

In our first lesson, we talked about King Saul and how he brought shame upon himself. Because he did not repent of his actions, the shame stayed with him. He continued to do things that were not pleasing to the Lord.

In **1 Samuel 15:2-5**, God tells Saul through the prophet, Samuel, to destroy the Amalekites. *"When the Israelites were on their way out of Egypt, the nation of Amalek attacked them. I am the LORD All-Powerful, and now I am going to make Amalek pay! Go and attack the Amalekites! Destroy them and all their possessions. Don't have any pity. Kill their men, women, children, and even their babies. Slaughter their cattle, sheep, camels, and donkeys. Saul sent messengers who told every town and* *village to send men to join the army at Telaim. There were two hundred ten thousand troops in all, and ten thousand of these were from Judah. Saul organized them, then led them to a valley near one of the towns in Amalek, where they got ready to make a surprise attack."* **(CEV)** The Amalekites had been very unkind to the Israelites and God was tired of it! He had decided to punish them, and He didn't want any trace of them left. God's instructions were very clear: <u>Kill everything</u>. <u>Destroy everything</u>. <u>Save nothing</u>.

So Saul got his troops together: a total of 210,000 men. **(1 Samuel 15:9 CEV)** *"Saul and his army let Agag live, and they also spared the best sheep and cattle. They didn't want to destroy anything of value, so they only killed the animals that were worthless or weak."* Did you hear what we just read? They didn't kill the best sheep or cattle, and they let the King of Amalek live! Saul just didn't get it, did he? Evidently, he had a big problem with pride; he couldn't seem to obey anything he was told to do! Needless to say, God was *not* happy! He talked to Samuel, the prophet, and said *"Saul has stopped obeying me, and I'm sorry that I made him king."* **(1 Samuel 15:11a CEV)**

Samuel went to see King Saul, who immediately began to make excuses for his actions. **(1 Samuel 15:16-23)** *"Stop! Samuel said. "Let me tell you what the LORD told me last night. All right, Saul answered. Samuel continued,"You may not think you're very important, but the LORD chose you to be king, and you are in charge of the tribes of Israel. When the LORD sent you on this mission, he told you to wipe out those worthless Amalekites. Why didn't you listen to the LORD? Why did you keep the animals and make him angry? But I did listen to the LORD! Saul answered. He sent me on a mission, and I went. I captured King Agag and destroyed his nation. All the animals were going to be destroyed anyway. That's why the army brought the best sheep and cattle to Gilgal as sacrifices to the LORD your God. Tell me, Samuel said. Does the LORD really want sacrifices and offerings? No! He doesn't want your sacrifices. He wants you to obey him. Rebelling against God or disobeying him because you are proud is just as bad as worshiping idols or asking them for advice. You refused to do what God told you, so God has decided that you can't be king."* **(CEV)**

God became so disgusted and angry with Saul over his disobedience that He was sorry He had chosen the man to be king over Israel. Because of this, God chose to remove His blessing from Saul's life! From this point, we see King Saul's behavior become much worse, because God was no longer watching out for him. The shame of it caused him to become a very angry and troubled person. Saul was too prideful to admit that he had been wrong (more than once). Every time he disobeyed, he tried to cover up his wrongdoing with excuses! He could not admit that he had sinned, that he had gone against what God wanted him to do.

God gave King Saul many chances to repent, but he simply would not do it. If he had only humbled himself before God and repented for his actions, God would have never removed His blessing from Saul's life. Instead, Saul carried the shame of knowing that he had disappointed God so badly that He completely forsook (deserted or left) Saul! Saul never overcame the shame, and he ended up taking his own life while his army was fighting a losing battle against the Philistines **(1 Samuel 31:2-4)**.

Remember, we're talking about shame. What are the two types of shame? (1) The shame that someone puts upon you, and (2) shame that you bring on yourself.

Saul is an example of what happens when a person allows shame to remain in their life. The devil will take advantage of whatever weakness we have. In Saul's case, the devil used his pride. If your weakness is anger, he will use that against you. If you feel badly because someone has said something to hurt you, the devil will constantly remind you of it. If you did something wrong and tried to hide it, the memory of it will trouble you. In time, you may be able to bury it way back in your mind, but it never really leaves. It will pop up when you least expect it, and with the memory comes the bad feelings that you had when it first happened. Our heart changes when we don't let God fix our hurts, because it restricts (or stops) our Holy Ghost from working in our lives.

We have learned about the two types of shame, and we have talked about the effects of shame in our life. Next week, we're going to identify what our shame is; then, we will have a time of prayer in order to get rid of it. I look forward to the great things God is going to do next week! Don't miss it!

SHAME LESSON #4:
How Does Shame Affect Me?

Lesson suggestion: *Whiteboard, markers. Invite experienced intercessors, who will understand the necessity of the healing taking place, to pray with the children at the close of class. Have adequate adult help so that each child is covered in prayer.*

This is our final lesson on "Shame." *We have said that there are two kinds of shame: (1) The shame that someone puts upon you, and (2) shame that you bring on yourself.* In the past several lessons, we have learned what shame is, and we have learned how Satan will use it against us. Today, we're going to identify our shame; then, we are going to work on getting rid of it.

In order to be set free from our shame, we must understand the difference between guilt and shame.

- "True guilt comes from God as our spirit is convicted for the wrong thing that we have done.
- Shame comes from the devil in the form of lies, which he uses to accuse us. We give Satan access to our heart when we carry grudges against others and ourselves.
- "Guilt is a sin that deserves blame or punishment.
- Shame is a feeling of self-rejection."[73] We feel this when we believe that we deserve a punishment.
- "Guilt says, "I have done wrong."
- Shame says, "I am wrong."
- Guilt says, "My behavior is not good."
- Shame says, "I am not good."
- Guilt says, "I have failed."
- Shame says, "I am a failure.""[74]

When we are willing to recognize and admit our guilt, God can help us with our shame. Remember, guilt is the conviction of the Holy Ghost that lets us know when we have done wrong. Once we repent, God forgives and forgets.

- **(2 Corinthians 7:10 NLT)** *"For God can use sorrow in our lives to help us turn away from sin and seek salvation. We will never regret that kind of sorrow."*
- **(Psalm 103:3 NLT)** *"He forgives all my sins."*
- **(Psalm 103:8-13 NLT)** *"The LORD is merciful and gracious; he is slow to get angry and full of unfailing love. He will not constantly accuse us, nor remain angry forever. He has not punished us for all our sins, nor does he deal with us as we deserve. For his unfailing love toward those who fear him is as great as the height of the heavens above the earth. He has removed our rebellious acts as far away from us as the east is from the west. The LORD is like a father to his children, tender and compassionate to those who fear him."*

We must have faith and believe that (1) God *has* the power to set us free, and that (2) He *will* set us free.

- **(2 Corinthians 5:17 CEV)** *"Anyone who belongs to Christ is a new person. The past is forgotten, and everything is new."*

---

[73] "Shame Book Series (The Shame Notebook), Book 8: "Ministering Deliverance and Healing to Shame" Antioch Publishes the Word 2001, Rev. Chester Wright.
[74] "Shame Book Series (The Shame Notebook), Book 8: "Ministering Deliverance and Healing to Shame" Antioch Publishes the Word 2001, Rev. Chester Wright.

Jesus understands shame, for He suffered shame Himself while He was on earth.

> 1. "He felt rejected and abandoned by His Father.
> 2. He was rejected by His people, His hometown, His leaders, His family, and His closest friends.
> 3. He was falsely accused and was called a liar.
> 4. His person was violated and He was physically, mentally, and emotionally abused.
> 5. He was let down and abandoned by all those that He did so much for.
> 6. He was publicly ridiculed and humiliated.
> 7. He was exposed naked before all.
> 8. He was accused pride and called a failure.
> 9. He was minimized and treated as less than He was.
> 10. He died innocent of all that He was charged with."[75]

(Isaiah 53:3-7 NLT) *"He was despised and rejected—a man of sorrows, acquainted with bitterest grief. We turned our backs on him and looked the other way when he went by. He was despised, and we did not care. Yet it was our weaknesses he carried; it was our sorrows that weighed him down. And we thought his troubles were a punishment from God for his own sins! But he was wounded and crushed for our sins. He was beaten that we might have peace. He was whipped, and we were healed! All of us have strayed away like sheep. We have left God's paths to follow our own. Yet the LORD laid on him the guilt and sins of us all. He was oppressed and treated harshly, yet he never said a word. He was led as a lamb to the slaughter. And as a sheep is silent before the shearers, he did not open his mouth."*

(Romans 8:35-39 NLT) *"Can anything ever separate us from Christ's love? Does it mean he no longer loves us if we have trouble or calamity, or are persecuted, or are hungry or cold or in danger or threatened with death? (Even the Scriptures say, "For your sake we are killed every day; we are being slaughtered like sheep.") No, despite all these things, overwhelming victory is ours through Christ, who loved us. And I am convinced that nothing can ever separate us from his love. Death can't, and life can't. The angels can't, and the demons can't. Our fears for today, our worries about tomorrow, and even the powers of hell can't keep God's love away. Whether we are high above the sky or in the deepest ocean, nothing in all creation will ever be able to separate us from the love of God that is revealed in Christ Jesus our Lord."*

Did you hear the last part of that verse? <u>*Nothing*</u> can separate us from God's love. In order to be set free from shame, we must do some very important things.

1. We must forgive ourselves.
2. We must forgive others.
3. We must forgive God.
4. We must ask God to forgive those who have hurt us.

In just a few minutes, we are going to have a special time of prayer. It is very important that you listen closely to what I am about to tell you. We will be handing out a card that will help you while you are praying. Because the way you are about to pray may be new to you, we want to help you all that we can. *(Teacher: hand out the cards and read them while the children follow along. Give an example of how they should pray, inserting verbal examples into the blanks provided. Have your intercessors ready to assist whenever needed.)* <u>The cards should not be filled out; they are for prayer help only.</u>

Instruct the students as follows:

"Forgiving is imperative" (a must), "even when it makes no sense and when you do not feel anything."[76] Tell them to think in this way:

---

[75] "Shame Book Series (The Shame Notebook), Book 8: "Ministering Deliverance and Healing to Shame" Antioch Publishes the Word 2001, Rev. Chester Wright.
[76] "Shame Book Series (The Shame Notebook), Book 8: "Ministering Deliverance and Healing to Shame" Antioch Publishes the Word 2001, Rev. Chester Wright.

1. "I must *forgive myself.*
2. I must *forgive (my) parents for dying, giving me up for adoption, etc.*
3. I must *forgive God* when it seems impossible for all things to work together for good.
4. I must ask the Lord to "lay not this sin to their charge.""[77]

The Spirit of the Lord will bring "buried" memories of hurt, pain, etc. to our conscious minds so that we may deal with them.

1. ""Any memory which provokes a *negative emotional reaction* is" (an unresolved) "issue from (our) past…Even if (we) have tried to deal with it before, the wound *is not* healed if the memory of it causes pain, shame, etc.
2. We can pray (in this way): "God, I forgive… help me to forgive … forgive through me.""[78]

"Forgiving is releasing the blame and letting it go to God. Forgiving is "giving up" control to God."[79] It allows us to get on with our life, setting aside those things that have hurt us. When we have been wounded, God gives us the Gift of Grief, which is the ability to grieve over our hurt. To "grieve" means *'To feel pain of mind or heart; to be in pain on account of an evil; to sorrow; to mourn.'*[80] Expressing our grief will cleanse the wound in our heart and cause it to heal. Our grief may feel like anger that we have kept pushed down inside of us for so long. It may be hard to let this anger come out, but we must do so in order for our wounds to heal. Once we allow our grief to release, God can heal us from our shame.

God is waiting to take your shame (your burden) away from you. **Matthew 11:28-30** says, *"Then Jesus said, "Come to me, all of you who are weary and carry heavy burdens, and I will give you rest. Take my yoke upon you. Let me teach you, because I am humble and gentle, and you will find rest for your souls. For my yoke fits perfectly, and the burden I give you is light."* **(NLT)**

(Revelation 3:20 NLT) *"Look! Here I stand at the door and knock. If you hear me calling and open the door, I will come in, and we will share a meal as friends."*

(Prepare for prayer time. Have adequate adult coverage so that each child is covered in prayer.)

---

[77] "Shame Book Series (The Shame Notebook), Book 8: "Ministering Deliverance and Healing to Shame" Antioch Publishes the Word 2001, Rev. Chester Wright. (words in parentheses added by author)
[78] "Shame Book Series (The Shame Notebook), Book 8: "Ministering Deliverance and Healing to Shame" Antioch Publishes the Word 2001, Rev. Chester Wright. (words in parentheses added by author)
[79] "Shame Book Series (The Shame Notebook), Book 8: "Ministering Deliverance and Healing to Shame" Antioch Publishes the Word 2001, Rev. Chester Wright.
[80] Noah Webster's 1828 Dictionary of American English

Teacher's Toolbox

Permission granted to reproduce the items in the Teacher's Toolbox as needed.

PRAYER WHEEL

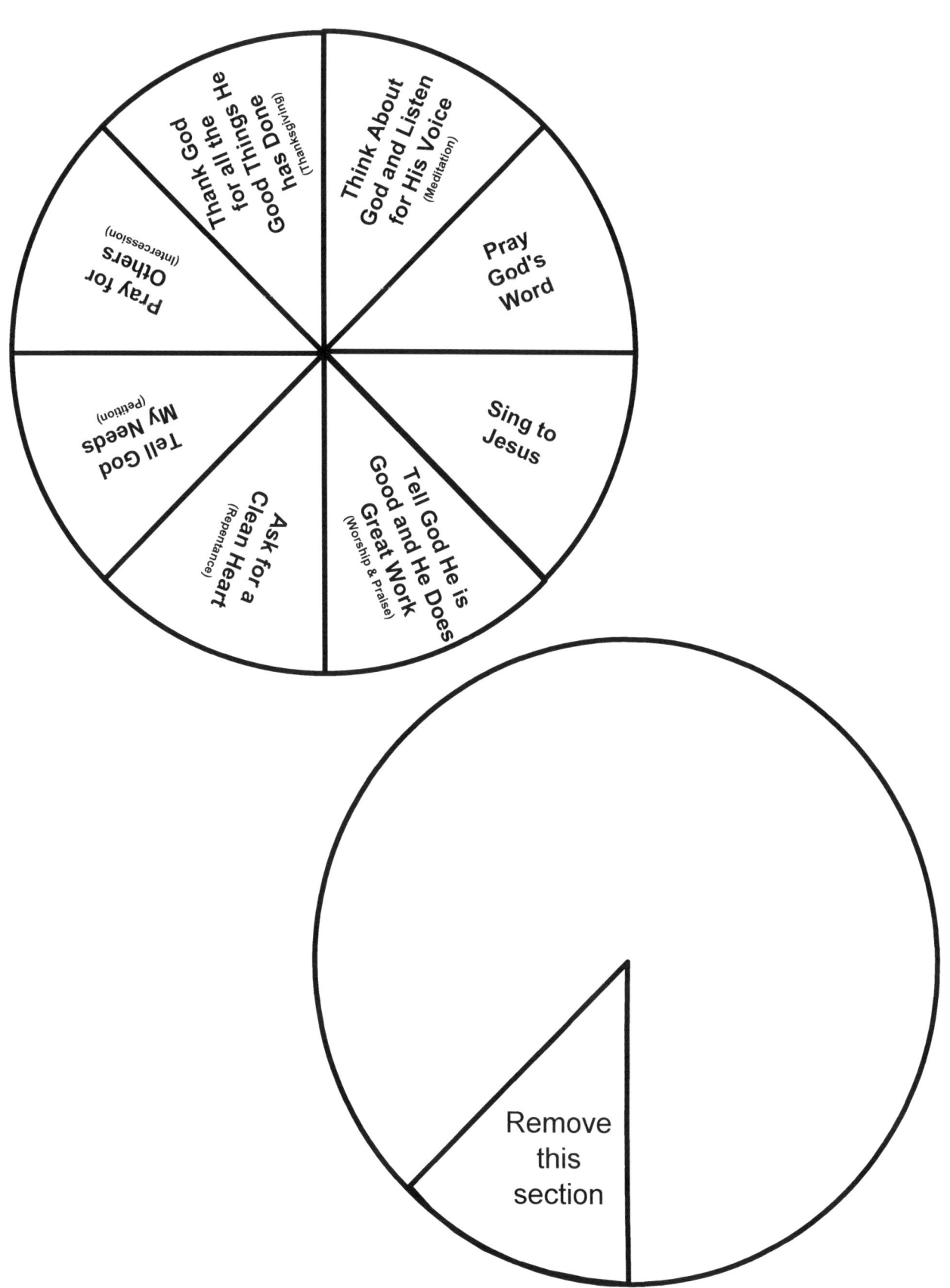

MY BIBLE STUDY FORM

Date:	1. Verse(s):
2. I prayed about the verse: ☐ (Check when finished)	
3. I think the verse(s) mean:	

4. I am going to use this verse to help me change:

4. I am going to memorize this verse(s): _____ (Write out scripture to memorize):

Please use additional pages (or the back of this page) if you need more room!

Prayer & Fasting Commitment Card

I will do my best to fast _____ for _____ days. I understand that by doing this, I will get to know God better. I will also do my best to pray for _____ minutes each day.

_____
Student Signature

_____
Date

Prayer & Fasting Commitment Card

I will do my best to fast _____ for _____ days. I understand that by doing this, I will get to know God better. I will also do my best to pray for _____ minutes each day.

_____
Student Signature

_____
Date

"21-DAYS MAKE A HABIT"
Prayer & Bible Reading Chart

My goal: To grow my relationship with God
I plan to: Pray and read the Bible *every day* for <u>21 days in a row</u>

- Choose a scripture passage of no less than 5 verses to read each day; then, write the reference on in the box provided. You can also write your references on the back of this paper, if necessary.
- Choose a "prayer minutes" goal, then stick to it every day!

I will pray at least_____ minutes a day. Start date: _____ End date: _____

Parent/Guardian: please initial in the shaded box marked "Done" after the daily goal is met.

Day 1	Day 2	Day 3	Day 4	Day 5	Day 6	Day 7
I prayed ___ minutes.	I prayed ___ minutes.	I prayed ___ minutes.	I prayed ___ minutes.	I prayed ___ minutes.	I prayed ___ minutes.	I prayed ___ minutes.
I read	I read	I read	I read	I read	I read	I read
Done:	Done:	Done:	Done:	Done:	Done:	Done:

Day 8	Day 9	Day 10	Day 11	Day 12	Day 13	Day 14
I prayed ___ minutes.	I prayed ___ minutes.	I prayed ___ minutes.	I prayed ___ minutes.	I prayed ___ minutes.	I prayed ___ minutes.	I prayed ___ minutes.
I read	I read	I read	I read	I read	I read	I read
Done:	Done:	Done:	Done:	Done:	Done:	Done:

Day 15	Day 16	Day 17	Day 18	Day 19	Day 20	Day 21
I prayed ___ minutes.	I prayed ___ minutes.	I prayed ___ minutes.	I prayed ___ minutes.	I prayed ___ minutes.	I prayed ___ minutes.	I prayed ___ minutes.
I read	I read	I read	I read	I read	I read	I read
Done:	Done:	Done:	Done:	Done:	Done:	Done:

USING THE 21-DAY-HABIT CHART

First, and most importantly, your students' parents need to be included at the start of this project; you may even want to hold a short informational meeting, or else give them a detailed explanation letter, including the prayer chart, prior to beginning. Without their knowledge and participation, there will more than likely not be great success in reaching the intended goal. If every parent is provided with an explanation of the process, what is expected of the child, and what help is needed from them as parents, the project's success rate will be much higher.

Make your rules clear, concise, and without deviations. If you make allowances for one child, you'll have to make allowances for all. The following guidelines are simply provided as ideas for you to consider. Whatever you do, *work to create excitement about building a prayer relationship with Jesus!* When your students grasp the importance – and power – of prayer, you will begin to see their lives flourish with spiritual growth!

Ideas for implementation

- Create contest teams
    - Split your age groups (e.g. ages 5-7 and 8-11). The vast ages represent an array of ability, and you want every student to gain knowledge from this! If you want to create even more competition, split the girls and boys into separate teams; then, divide those groups by age as well.
- Children should pray a minimum amount of minutes equal to their age (i.e. a 9-year-old should pray a minimum of 9 minutes). *However,* **please note:** *if this is your first prayer project with the children in your group, we recommend that you lower the minimum prayer time for all children. This will help ease them into their habit, rather than making it appear unattainable.* Should you have a child protest that it's not possible for them to do so, simply encourage them to try.
- Award a point for each minute prayed *over* their age (i.e. if a 9 year old prays 15 minutes, award 6 points).
- Award a point for each bible verse read. Ask that each child read at least 5 verses per day. If he/she cannot read, ask for someone to read to them.
- Award 5 points for each additional person who prays with them (i.e. if mom *and* dad pray with them, they get 10 points).
- Have your students turn in their chart even if all spaces are not filled in. Every effort counts!
- Consider awarding prizes for *Most Verses Read, Most Minutes Prayed, Best Overall Individual Achievement* (minutes prayed and verses read), *Highest Achieving Team Award* (pizza party or like event), and *a Consistency Award.*
- Our pastor provided platform time for our award ceremony, and we handed out our trophies during the Sunday evening service. You should have seen the smiles of the children as they heard their family and friends clap for them!
- The first year (prior to years two through five, when we gave trophies), we gave small candy bars to everyone who turned in a chart, incomplete or not. However, the ones who turned in a complete chart received the BIG candy bars, which made the other children decide that they would do better next time around!

These are just ideas to help you get started. As the teacher, you know best what will excite your children to participate! *Most importantly, do not get discouraged when a large number of your students don't finish all of the 21 days.* Sometimes, only 10 (out of 40-50) of our students would pray and read their Bible every day, generally due to a lack of parental support and involvement. However, we continued to offer the opportunity each January and August simply because we knew that there were those who were eager to learn. They were grasping the knowledge that we were pouring into them! Teacher, it *is* worth your effort!

Shame Prayer Card
(Not to be written on; for use as a prayer tool only)

Forgiving yourself
Jesus, with your help, I forgive and release myself for _____.

Forgiving others
Jesus, with your help, I forgive and release _____ for _____.

Forgiving God
Jesus, with your help, I forgive and release you for _____.

Pray each of these things as many times as you need to. God will bring each hurt to your mind as you pray. When something new comes to your thoughts, pray for it.

Shame Prayer Card
(Not to be written on; for use as a prayer tool only)

Forgiving yourself
Jesus, with your help, I forgive and release myself for _____.

Forgiving others
Jesus, with your help, I forgive and release _____ for _____.

Forgiving God
Jesus, with your help, I forgive and release you for _____.

Pray each of these things as many times as you need to. God will bring each hurt to your mind as you pray. When something new comes to your thoughts, pray for it.

PRAYER TIME IDEAS
We are very thankful for ideas that we have gleaned from others over the years!

CREATING A PRAYER BOX
Use a 3"x5" file card box. Purchase both lined and unlined file cards. You can also use dividers to separate the cards by type (such as families, missionaries, church leadership, etc.).

Prayer card ideas:

- Have the children bring in pictures of people that they know (e.g. unsaved family members: any and every one, such as immediate family, aunts, uncles, cousins, grandparents, unsaved teachers and friends, etc.). Glue the pictures to the file cards and label them with the person's name and need, along with the name of the child who is requesting prayer for them (*you will want to specify to the parents that the pictures will not be returned*).
- Make a card for the pastor, his wife, and each department leader in your local church.
- Have cards made for the organization's general assembly leadership, such as the General Superintendent, etc.
- Make a card with each missionary's name on it. Label with their name and the country they serve.
- Create a card for those persons you know who have a terminal illness. Pray diligently for their healing, and see what God will do!

This box can be used whenever you want to have focused prayer. You can also use it for prayer projects by selecting a section to concentrate on.

CREATING A PRAYER WHEEL
A reproducible copy of a "kid-based" prayer wheel has been included in this section.

<u>Create wheels to be used at church in your organized prayer times.</u>
We did this for our group; however, as our wheel's sections were in color, the cost for color copies was rather high. Because of this, our total project cost was just under $100; it is *not* necessary to be extravagant with the materials that you use.

- First, cut out circles of poster board slightly larger than the prayer wheel circle, and then glue a copy of the wheel onto it. Then, cut a circle (of the same size) for the top and remove a "slice" of it in order to reveal one section of the wheel at a time. Once this is complete, we suggest having the wheels laminated, as they will last longer. Laminating at either a school or office supply store is generally sold by the foot, and is usually inexpensive.
- After the lamination is complete, cut out the wheels and use brads to connect the two pieces.

<u>Give the children an opportunity to make, and take home, their own prayer wheels.</u>

- *Set aside a night for the children to make their own prayer wheels to take home. Obviously, you will not go to the expense on these that you would on the others, as you're not assured they won't be lost! You can also use slightly stronger-than-normal paper, and let the kids color their "pie sections." We also used different color paper for the top circle to make it a little more fun.*

TEACHING INTERCESSION USING THE FAMILY PHOTO ALBUM

- Everyone has unsaved family members. This idea can even be used in the home! Tell your students to ask their parents or guardian for family pictures. They can intercede for their aunts, uncles, cousins, grandparents, etc. as they look at the pictures.
- You could expand this by creating an album of your own! Ask your students to bring in pictures of their unsaved family and friends.
- Allocate a page to each child, allowing him or her to fill the page with pictures.

- Claim the individuals for Jesus; once someone receives salvation, you can either remove their picture, or place a smiley face sticker on it!
- You could also create a bulletin board (or album) that represents the "newly saved" loved ones for whom you have prayed!

MISSIONS-FOCUSED IDEAS

- Keep a globe handy in your prayer area. Select a child to begin, and have them spin the globe and select a spot upon it. Have the group pray for the selected country and the appointed missionary, if there is one. Take turns as long as time allows, or until you wish to change focus.
    - If a tabletop globe isn't available, obtain an inflatable one; then, have the children toss it to each other, designating the one with the ball as prayer leader. The leader selects a country, then leads the entire group in prayer.
- Have your church's Missions representative meet with the children once a month.
    - Assign at least one missionary to each child; then, give them a copy of the mission newsletters that the church receives from that particular family or individual. This allows them to keep up with the happenings in the country, as well as offering insight into the lives of the missionaries for whom they are praying.

SOME RECOMMENDED READING

- *Let the Children Pray* (Guidelines for parents and children's ministries on teaching children to pray), by Fredi Trammel.
- *Children of Revival: Letting the Little Ones Lead,* by Vann Lane (Children's Pastor of Brownsville Assembly of God) –an inspiring book that tells about the children's role in the Brownsville Revival.
- *The Prayer Journey for KIDS,* by Fredi Trammel. This is a terrific resource *for your children.*
- *Children Intercessors Army: The Children's Guide to Spiritual Warfare,* by Fredi Trammel; this is another awesome resource *for your children.*

ABOUT THE AUTHORS

Mark and Glenda Alphin have both been involved in multiple facets of ministry throughout their lives, but children's ministry stands out simply because it played a great role in preparation for their current responsibilities.

Glenda began ministering to children as a Sunday School teacher during her late teen years. At *The Church Triumphant of Columbus*, she taught 5-6 year-olds for 9 years; simultaneously, she also served as Assistant Sunday School Superintendent. During part of those 9 years, Mark led Children's Outreach, drove the church van on Sunday mornings, and assisted the Sunday School department with special activities. Additionally, he served as a substitute Sunday School teacher.

Beginning in 2000, they co-led a children's group called *Warriors in Training* for 5 years, which was birthed from a burden to instill Apostolic doctrine within the children of their local assembly. Their pastor, Rev. William L. Sciscoe, saw the need as presented, and enabled Mark and Glenda to create and grow this brand-new ministry within the church, even personally reading and approving every lesson. The burden came to fruition, a vision was realized, and the result is what you now hold in your hand: an Apostolic, doctrinal resource written specifically for children being raised in Oneness Apostolic churches and homes.

In 2005, along with the Alphin family, the *Growing with God* curriculum made its way across the waters and was shared with multiple missionaries, which resulted in its Russian translation. Later, during their first mission term in Finland, the Alphins began sharing this very curriculum with brand-new adult converts.

To God be the glory for what *He* has done!

Made in the USA
San Bernardino, CA
19 August 2016